Making Friends, Making Disciples

Growing Your Church through Authentic Relationships

LEE B. SPITZER

J. DWIGHT STINNETT, SERIES EDITOR

Living Church

Making Friends, Making Disciples
Growing Your Church through Authentic Relationships

Interior design by Wendy Ronga at Hampton Design Group (www.hamptondesigngroup.com).
Cover design by Tobias Becker and Birdbox Graphic Design (www.birdboxdesign.com).

Library of Congress Cataloging-in-Publication Data
Spitzer, Lee B.
Making friends, making disciples: growing your church through authentic relationships/Lee B. Spitzer.—1st ed. p. cm.—(Living church series) Includes bibliographical references. ISBN 978-0-8170-1645-6 (pbk.: alk. paper)
1. Church growth. 2. Interpersonal relations—Religious aspects—Christianity. 3. Discipling (Christianity) I. Title.
BV652.25.S65 2010 254'.5—dc22 2010021828

Printed in the U.S.A.
First Edition, 2010.

Contents

Preface to the Series

"What happened? Just a few years ago we were a strong church. We had thriving ministries and supported a worldwide mission effort. Our community knew us and cared about what we did. Now we're not sure if we can survive another year."

It is a painful conversation I have had with more church leaders than I can name here.

I explained how images such as *meltdown*, *tsunami*, *earthquake*, and *storm* have been used to describe the crisis developing in the North American church over the last 25 years. Our present crisis is underscored by the American Religious Identification Survey 2008. Not just one local congregation, but nearly every church is being swamped by the changes.

Volumes have already been written in analysis of the current situation and in critique of the church. I suggested a few books and workshops that I knew, trying to avoid the highly technical works. But the church leader with whom I was talking was overwhelmed by all the analysis. "Yes, I am sure that is true. But what do we do? When I look at what is happening and I hear all the criticism, I wonder if the church has a future at all. Do we deserve one?"

I emphasized that there are no simple answers and that those who offer simplistic solutions are either deceived or deceiving. There is no "church cookbook" for today (and I'm not sure there ever really was one). I tried to avoid an equally simplistic pietistic answer.

Still, the church leader pressed. "So is the church dead? Do we just need to schedule a funeral and get over it? We are all so tired and frustrated."

I do not accept the sentiment of futility and despair about the future of the church. I believe the church is alive and persists not because of what we do, but because of what God has done and continues to do in the church.

The pain is real, however, as are the struggle and the longing. I wanted to help church leaders such as this one understand, but not be overwhelmed by the peculiar set of forces impacting the church today. But information was not enough. I wanted to encourage them with specific things that can be done, without implying that success is guaranteed or that human effort is sufficient. I wanted them to learn from what others are doing, not to copy them mechanically, but to use what others are doing as eyeglasses to look closely at their own context. I wanted them to avoid all the churchy labels that are out there, and be a living church in their community, empowered and sustained by the living God.

Those of us who work with groups of churches and who pay attention to the things that are happening around us know that several forces are having a devastating affect on the church today. Both formal studies and personal observation identify at least eight key areas where the impact has been especially acute. These areas are biblical illiteracy, financial pressures, overwhelming diversity, shrinking numbers, declining leadership base, brokenness in and around us, narrowing inward focus, and unraveling of spiritual community. It is not hard to see how each of these is related to the others.

Living Church is a new series from Judson Press intended to address each of these forces from a congregational perspective. While our authors are well-informed biblically, theologically, and topically, these volumes are not intended to be an exercise in ecclesiastical academics. Our intent is to empower congregational leaders (both clergy and laity) to rise to the challenge before us.

Our goal is not merely to lament our state of crisis, but to identify creative and constructive strategies for our time and place so that we can move on to effective responses. Our time and place is the American church in the twenty-first century.

My good friend, Rev. Dr. Lee Spitzer, has launched this series with the volume *Making Friends, Making Disciples: Growing Your Church through Authentic Relationships*. While this book addresses the issue of shrinking numbers, it is not a church-growth manual, an evangelism strategy, or a church marketing guide.

Lee gets to the heart of the matter, asserting that the church is a Christ-centered community of friends that is committed to making more friends. His approach goes much deeper than "friendship evangelism." Lee explores "how friendship informs the internal life (discipleship) and outreach ministry (evangelism in a holistic sense) of the church in the twenty-first century." He argues powerfully that cultivating friendship with God and neighbor is a spiritual discipline, not having some ulterior motive, but because God has called us to make and be friends.

In this tour of friendship, Lee takes a look at both the contributions and dangers of social networking and other modern technologies. With his paradigm of "friendship circles," he challenges the church to practice robust friendship in a culture that increasingly trivializes friendship.

Making Friends, Making Disciples is a good beginning for a living church—learning again how to be friends with God and with one another.

—Rev. Dr. J. Dwight Stinnett
Series Editor
Executive Minister
American Baptist Churches, Great Rivers Region

Acknowledgments

I would like to dedicate this book to Rev. Howard and Hazel Keeley, two of the closest friends Lois and I have ever had. For thirty years they have loved us and made us a part of their family. As my mentor, Howard has shared his wisdom and pastoral expertise with me. He introduced me to American Baptist life and officiated at my ordination service. It was a privilege to serve as his youth minister at Trinity Baptist Church in Lynnfield, Massachusetts, and later to succeed him as senior pastor of the First Baptist Church in Lincoln, Nebraska. I am blessed to be able to call him my friend.

I thank God for the many friends with whom I've shared life's journey. Special thanks to my close friends who helped edit and shape this book: my best friend and wife, Lois; Rev. Ann and Bruce Borquist; Mrs. Sandy Denton; Rev. Dr. Frank Reeder; Rev. Dr. Elmo Familiaran; Rev. Vern Mattson; and again, Rev. Howard Keeley. Thanks for reading not only my words, but also my heart!

Finally, a word of thanksgiving and appreciation to the American Baptist Churches of New Jersey, a regional fellowship that is striving to become more spiritually healthy and faithful. What a joy it is to serve as your executive minister and senior regional pastor! I also work with a wonderful ministry team, and I thank God for you all!

—Rev. Dr. Lee B. Spitzer
Thanksgiving Day 2009

Introduction

"Though we are nineteen clicks away from everybody on the Web, we are only one click away from our friends."[1]
—Albert-László Barabási, *Linked*

On an ideal Saturday, I wake up just after the sun rises. Before reaching the kitchen, I exit the house to scoop up the day's *Wall Street Journal*, and return to pour fresh coffee into my favorite mug.

Over that first cup of coffee, I peruse the newspaper and snip several articles for further review. Then I try to read more news online. But sooner or later—usually sooner—curiosity overcomes me, and I check to see if I have received any significant e-mails overnight. Then I check Flickr.com to see if friends have posted new photos, and finally, move onto Facebook and respond to two or three notes there. Later, I will talk with a friend on Skype; I'm looking forward to seeing him as we catch up.

Although I am an introvert who prizes his privacy and prefers conversation with one or two friends to a party room filled with dozens, this ritual of connection and support gives me energy and joy each day. And I know I am not alone in this feeling.

Friendship and Church Life in a Connected World

In a postmodern and high-tech age characterized by both unprecedented digital connectivity and personal isolation, friendship is on everyone's mind. Social networking websites are the hottest sites on the Internet. Facebook now boasts some 300 million users[2]—nearly matching the total population of the United States! Twenty-first century technology has shrunk the world so it can fit on your computer or cell phone screen.

How should we respond to the opportunities and challenges posed by the technological advances that are transforming human communications, relationships, and culture around the globe? For almost two thousand years, the Christian church has led the way in creating community. Can we discover a transformative paradigm for church growth—not only in terms of the number of people who join but also in regard to the maturity of disciples who participate in the life of the church?

The key is to visualize how friendship interfaces with the church's call to be a community of faith-filled disciples seeking to share the good news of Jesus Christ with their friends, acquaintances, and others. Friendship, community, discipleship, evangelism, and social witness all play starring roles in the church's fulfillment of God's will.

Friendship Is "the Secret of the Universe"

Any serious study of friendship must begin by recognizing that a standard definition of *friendship* does not exist! In *Simple Words*, the distinguished Jewish scholar Rabbi Adin Steinsaltz examines the meaning of a host of common terms—such as *nature, good, faith,* and *death*—to reveal wisdom about how humans see themselves. Sandwiched between chapters on masks and family, he probes the meaning of the word *friends.* Steinsaltz writes: "The term 'friendship' does not have an exact, universal meaning. Its precise definition may be, like pornography, a matter of geography, and indeed, its meaning varies from country to country and from culture to culture."[3]

We may not agree on a universal definition, yet friendship captures the hearts of all who dare to imagine that we can transcend loneliness and solitude. Henry David Thoreau wrote: "No word is oftener on the lips of men than Friendship, and indeed no thought is more familiar to their aspirations. All men are dreaming of it, and its drama, which is always a tragedy, is enacted daily. It is the secret of the universe."[4]

If friendship is, indeed, "the secret of the universe," then it's not surprising we can find no simple, universally shared understanding of the term. But let's not be too quick to abandon the search! Exemplifying the best of Jewish wisdom seeking, Rabbi Steinsaltz asks us all to spend a little more time examining the issue so that we can create a paradigm of friendship. Having made allowances for cultural and historical differences, the rabbi calls us to consider the creation of a framework for defining friendship:

> The process of clarifying the meaning of friendship draws an outline, explores the boundaries of what exists, and creates the framework for developing the potential within the friendship…Without this process of recognizing, defining, and naming, if the friendship happens at all, it happens by chance. If so, it may not be appreciated until after it is gone, and the difference between "an acquaintance" and "a friend" realized only after the fact.[5]

Having made an impassioned case for a deeper examination of the definition of friendship, the rabbi returns to the crucial question and supplies an answer that serves as the key presupposition of this book:

> What, then, is the essence of friendship? It is the voluntary sharing with another of things that are important for me, whether it is sharing my possessions or my persona, my time or my secrets. In fact, the sharing does not always mean giving, but rather it is the will to allow somebody else to participate in something that is dear to me.[6]

A Journey of Sharing—and a Shared Journey

Both Thoreau and Steinsaltz bring to the fore important aspects of authentic friendship. When Thoreau writes, "O my friend, may it come to pass, once, that when you are my friend I may be yours,"[7] he rightly highlights the yearning we have for mutually satisfying companionship with others. We want to share life with those we love and appreciate. Most of life's events are richer when we experience them with people close to us, or share our stories with those who care enough to listen closely to us.

However, if we view friendship only as a mutual admiration society, we risk falling into an abyss of narcissism. If two people truly hope to experience the depths of authentic friendship, then they must recognize that their relationship does not exist in a vacuum. Friendship is not an end in itself, but rather it has meaning only in relation to our social context. Thoreau might exclaim, "Friendship is first, Friendship last"[8]—but most of us would recognize that, like most everything else that is good in this world, true friendship gives birth to something of worth and significance that moves us beyond ourselves. The love between a husband and a wife often leads to the birth of a child; in Christian cosmology, the eternal love that exists within the Trinity gives birth to a universe of diversity and beauty. In a similar way, all authentic friendships should give something back to a world that made it possible for those friendships to exist in the first place.

Steinsaltz has wisely pointed out that friendship must have a purpose in order to be meaningful. In Christian terms, we would say that *purpose and meaning are found in the fulfillment of God's will, and that God's will is expressed in and through our spiritual journeys lived out under the Lordship of Jesus Christ.* Accordingly, in this book we will explore the dimensions of friendship within the context of the church, the spiritual body of Christ. Christ's presence in our world is embodied in local congregations in which people called to do God's will journey together and find companionship, encouragement, and needed life resources.

Friendship is a journey of sharing between two or more people. No one can journey through life completely alone. Linking our lives through relationships permits us to share our hearts with others who, in turn, reveal themselves to us. When this is done in a free, healthy, and positive context, it is more satisfying than almost any other human interpersonal experience. To be loved and accepted—and to respond in kind—is at the very heart of what it means to be a human created in the image of God.

Friendship is also a shared journey in which we combine forces with others to fulfill God's will. Sharing events and experiences is an integral aspect of friendship. But deep friendship moves beyond leisure activities, encouraging partners to reach their creative potential, to serve others with resolve and hope, and to make the world a better place. Friendships change history in both small and large ways.

I found myself mulling over the meaning of friendship as I was preparing for a summer 2009 research sabbatical focused on love, friendship, and mission. With the support of my denomination's Board of International Ministries, I explored this theme with American Baptist missionaries on five continents. In preparation for my meetings with these missionaries, I felt it was important to try all the exercises I was planning to put them through. One exercise was straightforward: based on your experience, define *friendship* in two sentences or less. Having spent more than two decades reflecting on the meaning of friendship, I thought I could make short shrift of this exercise. Three hours later, after multiple revisions, I finally settled on the following definition:

> *A friend is a person I love who also loves me—through our linked journeys, bonds of devotion, affection, loyalty, trust, and caring grow between us, so that we desire to*

> *share our hopes, dreams, joys, and fears with each other. My friends exert influence over my heart; the deeper our friendship, the more vulnerable and self-revealing I am willing to be, and the more their opinions and feelings about me affect me.*

After listening to Thoreau and Steinsaltz, I would like to amend the definition by adding a third sentence: *Together with my friends, I hope to fulfill God's will for the church and change the world for Christ.*

Reaching for the Great Prize of Genuine Friends

Steinsaltz observes that "finding a genuine friend is a great prize."[9] Friendship is, indeed, a great prize. This is why, when we seek to describe the intimacy of our relationship with Christ, we often use the language of friendship. We sing and cherish hymns such as "What a Friend We Have in Jesus." Our hearts stir when we hear Jesus' words, "I do not call you servants any longer ... but I have called you friends" (John 15:15). We understand that friendship—with Christ and with one another—has the power to transform us and our world.

In this book, we will explore how friendship informs the internal life (discipleship) and outreach ministry (evangelism in a holistic sense) of the church in the twenty-first century. The first three chapters are foundational to our discussion. In chapter one, we will identify loneliness as the primary challenge to human happiness and explore its implications for the church. In chapter two, we will examine how Jesus understood and practiced the art of friendship. In chapter three, we will widen our investigation to develop a theology of friendship based on the totality of biblical teaching.

In chapter four, we will explore how friendship may be defined within the context of the church's life and mission. How do we move beyond *friendliness* to *deep friendship* as the people of God?

In chapter five, we will introduce the *Friendship Circles* model for appreciating our friends; and in chapter six, we will probe how our friendship circles may impact all aspects of a congregation's spiritual journey.

Chapters seven through ten explore how we may practice friendship as a personal and corporate spiritual discipline. In chapter seven, we will explore how the ties of friendship circles impact discipleship and evangelism, and we'll discuss two knotty issues—friendships with non-Christians and friendships with persons of the opposite sex. Chapter eight offers a paradigm for a spirituality of friendship, while chapter nine offers advice on how the church can practice friendship as a spiritual discipline. In chapter ten, we acknowledge that friendships do end, and offer practical counsel on how to negotiate this aspect of our journeys.

We'll conclude with an optimistic look forward to the next one hundred years of friendship, considering how churches and individuals can grow toward the cutting edge of healthy and faithful relationships. And since I hope you will want to put into practice the principles and insights conveyed throughout the book, an appendix featuring nine key friendship circles exercises is included for your personal and church group use.

As we embark upon this journey, I hope each chapter will stimulate your thinking and help you grow in your appreciation of friendship. Let's begin by confronting friendship's foe—loneliness.

CHAPTER 1

Our Problem Is Loneliness

"Isolation, a sense of lack of profound contact with other human beings, seems to be the disease of our time."[1]
—Allan Bloom, *Love and Friendship*

Isolation, alienation, and estrangement from others have been a part of human life since the beginning of our species. The first human couple rebels against God's will, and becomes alienated from their Creator (Genesis 2–3). In just a short time, this spiritual divorce spills over into their relationship with each other, and the alienation is amplified in the next generation—when the first murder in the Bible is recorded (Genesis 4:1-16). We have never recovered from this relational disaster! In fact, humanity's sense of isolation has become more magnified. Allan Bloom writes that we have become a species of "social solitaries," yet we remain dissatisfied with this isolation:

> Nevertheless the most insistent demand nowadays of people in general, and young people in particular, remains human connection, a connection that transcends the isolation of personal selfishness, and in which the thought of oneself is inextricably bound up with the thought of another.[2]

The great paradox of our times is that technology has connected the whole world while leaving largely untouched the existential need of our hearts to be appreciated and loved. YouTube and a host of other websites have given us unparalleled opportunities to expose ourselves to the rest of the world. A well-placed video, blog entry, or musical clip may catapult us from obscurity to worldwide attention (for at least a news cycle or two), but little lasting satisfaction can be gained from such notoriety. Our hearts yearn for more authentic and enduring relational experiences that truly honor who we are. A keyboard cannot cure our loneliness, and our alienation cannot be bridged by a high-speed cable modem.

Authors John T. Cacioppo and William Patrick have observed:

> Almost everyone feels the pangs of loneliness at certain moments. It can be brief and superficial—being the last one chosen for a team on the playground—or it can be acute and severe—suffering the death of a spouse or a dear friend. Transient loneliness is so common, in fact, that we simply accept it as a part of life.[3]

Loneliness is a universal and pervasive problem in the twenty-first century. Not even the Christian church, the body of Christ, is exempt from this condition.

"American Loneliness" and the Church

In her novel, *Loss of Flight,* Sara Vogan introduces us to Dr. Max Bodine, a psychologist who pays house calls on his patients. During yet another session with Thomas, a longtime client, Dr. Bodine concludes: "It soon became apparent Thomas didn't want therapy as much as he simply wanted someone to talk to. American loneliness. A man with money and power and no one to talk to."[4]

Thomas may be a fictional client, but his plight rings true. *American loneliness.* Church pews are filled with people just like Thomas—strangers sitting alongside one another while worshiping a personal God who desires to be close to them all.

My father was one of the walking lonely toward the end of his life. A gregarious man, he was widowed in midlife. He never remarried, but thrived on the friends he made through his church on Long Island. Unfortunately, after retiring, my dad moved to Florida, where he never succeeded in finding a fully satisfying new web of relationships. When he died, I came into contact with his doctors, creditors, and bankers. From their stories, I was able to get a deeper sense of how my father spent his day. He created a routine to keep busy, and used his visits to them as substitutes for the social life he otherwise lacked.

Pastors encounter people who come to them with problems that may or may not require therapy. Yet in reality, many of these people come simply to be in the presence of a friendly face, to talk to someone who will give them the time of day, to share emotions of the heart or thoughts of the soul with someone who will take them seriously. Those who don't have a pastor to talk with may turn to a doctor, their banker, the beautician, a bartender, or a stranger on a bus or a park bench.

But it's not just lay members of our congregations who struggle with loneliness. A missionary recently said to me, "Missionaries and pastors are surrounded by people all the time and yet we are lonely. It's like we're swimming in the middle of a huge lake but dying of thirst."

In highlighting "American loneliness," Sara Vogan points to the link between the wealth and material progress of our country and the particular way the global malady of loneliness is often expressed in the United States. Alongside the creation of amazing wealth, Americans, Western Europeans, and other economically developed societies have experienced a growth in individualism and freedom. This has been accompanied by the elevation of the values of self-expression and personal creativity. Who can argue against individualism and freedom, or self-expression and personal creativity? These are all good.

However, we have also exposed ourselves to a kind of loneliness and alienation that more traditional societies did not necessarily have to contend with—at least not on the level that we face it. The freedom to travel and move wherever and whenever we wish, accompanied by high divorce rates and the demise of the nuclear and extended family, have created a situation in which we can be surrounded by people and yet still be lonely. One response to this isolation is the increasing reliance on technology to create surrogate forms of community, such as Facebook and MySpace.

I would argue that the Christian church has within it the potential to combat loneliness on a level that most other social communities cannot reach. This book is devoted to elucidating how the church can become the kind of community where loneliness can be effectively addressed.

If Loneliness Is the Problem, What's the Solution?

After thirty years of local church and regional pastoral ministry, I am convinced that loneliness—the absence of friends who attend to one's personal thoughts, dreams, hopes, and fears—is an epidemic affecting many of the people who listen to pastors preach on Sunday mornings. Is a sermon a good substitute for personal conversation? Does singing alongside others make up for having no one to eat lunch with? How does the church minister to a condition of the soul like loneliness? I would suggest a five-fold response—REACH:

Recognize the nature of the problem.

Explore emerging new possibilities in light of technological advances and cultural shifts.

Ask the right questions.

Create innovative friendship-focused models to line up our journeys with the challenges we face.

Help others apply these models and their wisdom to their own life situations, and to the life and ministries of their churches.

Recognize the Nature of the Problem—The church sometimes acts like it can cure loneliness. During the initial months of my first pastorate in East Providence, Rhode Island, a thrice-divorced woman in her forties joined my church and asked for my blessing to start a singles ministry for the community at large. She convinced me that such a group could serve as a healer of loneliness by providing a group of friends for single adults. I was overjoyed, because it seemed like a great way to reach out to people who were not part of our small church. Within three weeks, the singles ministry meetings had over forty people in attendance—more than attended our Sunday morning worship services! My euphoria (and dreams of a spectacular revival) soon ebbed as the people quickly paired off and then ceased coming. I had hoped the group could make people feel more comfortable with their singleness so they could focus on other parts of their lives; instead, it functioned as a dating service. Those who were unsuccessful in finding an appealing dating prospect quickly abandoned the group. Within three months, the ministry was defunct.

Loneliness will not be "fixed." The feeling of isolation comes from a complex confluence of personal, social, and spiritual factors. Cacioppo and Patrick rightly point out that loneliness is not a medical or even psychological problem begging for an antidote or cure. It operates more like an invitation to embrace new possibilities in life:

> Some individuals caught in the feedback loop of loneliness and negative affect, when they begin to focus on changing their social perceptions and behaviors, might benefit from medications to first bring their depression or anxiety under control. But once again, loneliness itself is not a disease; feeling lonely from time to time is like feeling hungry or thirsty from time to time. It is part of being human. The trick is to heed these signals in ways that bring long-term satisfaction.[5]

C.S. Lewis, coming from a more theological perspective, concurs: "As soon as we are fully conscious we discover loneliness."[6] Loneliness is a natural condition in life that serves to frame our spiritual journeys. People may be lonely for a variety of reasons:

- Our shyness, insecurities, or reserved personalities may discourage us from initiating friendships.
- Our commitment to work, families, or other organizations may rob of us of the time needed to maintain friendships.
- Memories of past rejections, unhealthy relationships, or the loss of past friends may hinder our enthusiasm to take new relational risks.
- We may have settled for having a large number of superficial relationships instead of focusing on a smaller set of more qualitatively significant friendships.
- Life's transitions may have depleted our pool of friendships. We may have moved to a new neighborhood, new job, new school, or new church. In doing so, we left friends behind.

None of these reasons for loneliness offers any indication that we are psychologically unhealthy, but each may cause us pain and suffering if not addressed appropriately.

Explore Emerging New Possibilities in Light of Technological Advances and Cultural Shifts—In September 2009, the Annual Session of the American Baptist Churches of New Jersey was a wonderful expression of the multicultural nature of the twenty-first-century church. Our Filipino council president welcomed delegates from African American, Eurocentric Anglo, Latino, Brazilian, Haitian, and Korean churches. The presidents of two overseas Baptist bodies were in attendance. But what really made it a watershed event for our regional family was that the plenary sessions were broadcast live over the Internet. People from nine countries and half a dozen other

U.S. states watched the sessions take place. Our statewide event was global, with almost 20 percent of those "attending" doing so online! The technology for the broadcast was provided by one of our "local" congregations—a church that broadcasts its services and events every day, reaching people all over the world.

Technology is changing the way we make friends, maintain relationships with existing friends, and serve others in the name of Jesus Christ! Paul employed an innovative approach to reaching new people for Christ and for encouraging existing disciples—the apostolic ministry journey. In the twenty-first century we can replicate his outreach without ever leaving home! People from more than 150 countries currently reside in New Jersey, making it easier than ever to help fulfill the Great Commission without extensive travel. The global reach of the Internet is transforming Christian witness and service.

Social networking sites such as Facebook are making it possible to stay in touch with hundreds of people, regardless of geographical proximity. Specialized sites such as Flickr (for photography enthusiasts) combine social networking with particular interests. Internet-based phone services such as Skype represent a giant leap in connecting people, making audio and video conversations (for both personal and conference calls) convenient and often free.

The church is just beginning to explore the possibilities inherent in these innovations. For example, in the past, pastors and deacons had to personally visit or telephone church members to stay in touch with them. These were time-consuming endeavors, with frustration built in—knocking on doors when no one is home, or calling people at inconvenient times for them to converse. With Facebook, a pastor or pastoral volunteer can keep in touch with her or his members with much less effort. A steady stream of personal information is pushed to us, and we can respond as needed. In the time it once took to say hello to one member, we can now catch up with dozens of people. Although they are not a replacement for face-to-face contact, social networking sites enable us to keep abreast of what is happening throughout the church community we belong to and serve.

Ask the Right Questions—Perhaps you're surprised to see this suggestion as the third step of our process, but asking questions necessarily comes after a preliminary gathering of data and trends. Having recognized the nature of loneliness and explored some promising possibilities for responding, we can now assemble a list of questions to guide our reflections.

Letty Cottin Pogrebin was motivated to write her book *Among Friends* by a riveting dinner-party conversation initiated by the great actor Alan Alda. As he prepared to film *The Four Seasons*, a movie about friendship, Alda hosted a dinner in which he asked those present to reflect on a number of questions about the nature of their friendships, including: What do you look for in a friend? How many really good friends do you have? Do you keep making new ones? Is there such a thing as having too many friends? Are you a good friend to the friends in your life? Did you ever lose a meaningful friend?[7]

In response to the conversation that ensued, Pogrebin mused: "Clearly, if this group was at all typical, being friends is not an instinct; it doesn't come naturally. What's more, being friends is not enough. We want to understand the meaning of friendship, the expectations friends have of each other, other people's ideas of 'too little' or 'enough.'"[8]

Although this book is focused primarily on how friendships influence and affect the church's work of evangelism and discipleship, I want to explore similar questions regarding the meaning and possibilities of authentic Christian friendship:

- How does friendship affect the way we fulfill the Great Commission and live out our calling to be Christ's witnesses and ambassadors of reconciliation?

- How does friendship relate to the journey God calls each Christian to embrace and fulfill?
- How does friendship shape and express the spiritual journey of the church?
- To what extent does friendship influence how we facilitate discipleship by empowering others to become friends of Jesus Christ?

Create Innovative Friendship-Focused Models of Church Life and Mission—In this book, we will consider three innovative perspectives for appreciating how friendships shape the church's call to evangelize and disciple.

First, my *Friendship Circles* model (on page 56) is a stimulating reflection tool that maps how close people are to our hearts. Cacioppo and Patrick speak of three "categories of social connection: intimate connectedness, relational connectedness, and collective connectedness."[9] Human beings need all these connections—with a significant other, child, or intimate companion; with a circle of extended family and friends; and with a network of belonging, such as a community of faith. The *Friendship Circles* model will help us see how we may advance the causes of evangelism and discipleship in a manner that is relationally positive and intentional.

Second, the *Church Health and Faithfulness* Survey methodology (see chapter 6) helps churches appreciate how far they have come in creating internally healthy congregations that serve their communities in a faithful manner. Recognizing that friendships both shape and are shaped by the social environments we belong to and serve, this survey will help us learn how our friendships interact with the fourteen themes that define congregational health and faithfulness.

Third, my *Endless Possibilities* spiritual journey paradigm (see chapter 6) demonstrates how God guides individuals and churches so that we may embrace, live out, and fulfill God's will. This paradigm focuses on the themes of our journeys, which are particular representations of God's will (journey goals). It focuses on how we can make progress in negotiating the five phases of each of our journeys. The *Endless Possibilities* paradigm applies to both individual journeys and the shared journey of a group (such as a congregation), and fully integrates the joys and challenges of friendship into its perspective.[10]

Help the Church Apply Models and Wisdom—We do not have to journey alone through this life. Whether we are single or married, at the beginning of life's adventure, in the middle, or nearing the end, God links our journeys to the journeys of other people who have also heard God's call.

We find lessons about loneliness and friendship—and how both are experienced in and through our spiritual journeys—throughout the Bible. For example, after his great victory over the prophets of Baal atop Mt. Carmel, the prophet Elijah fled for his life in response to the death threats of the treacherous Jezebel. Isolated and alone, Elijah falls into depression, and he expresses his misery in pitiful terms: "It is enough; now, O LORD, take away my life, for I am no better than my ancestors" (1 Kings 19:4). Even after an angel from God supplies him with bread and water so that he might gain strength for his journey to Mt. Horeb (19:7-8), Elijah complains about being lonely: "I alone am left, and they are seeking my life, to take it away" (19:10; see also 19:14). God then reveals that Elijah is not really alone; there are seven thousand other faithful Israelites (19:18). Soon after, Elijah's journey is linked to Elisha, who becomes his attendant and companion (19:19-21). The journey continues, but Elijah is no longer alone.

Elijah's concern was not just theological in nature—it was also intensely personal and practical. He was tired of feeling isolated; he wanted companions on his spiritual quest. Understanding Elijah's need and God's response encourages us to grow in our appreciation of the friends God has given to us and to pay particular attention to discerning the joys and responsibilities of being a friend. It also can give churches guidance and direction for creating authentic communities of faith where friendships flourish and guests are welcomed and invited to share in the richness of the kingdom of God.

Jesus and Loneliness

Jesus no doubt empathized with Elijah, for he also encountered rejection and isolation. Isaiah prophesied that the suffering Messiah would experience loneliness:

> For he grew up before him like a young plant, and like a root out of dry ground; he had no form or majesty that we should look at him, nothing in his appearance that we should desire him. He was despised and rejected by others; a man of suffering and acquainted with infirmity; and as one from whom others hide their faces he was despised, and we held him of no account. (Isaiah 53:2-3)

In Gethsemane, Jesus prayed alone while the disciples slept nearby (Matthew 26:36-46). Though spectators gawked and friends kept their distance, Jesus endured a hasty trial, suffered punishment at the hands of Roman soldiers, and died on the cross—a single sacrificial lamb for the sins of the whole world (John 1:29). Author Shusaku Endo describes how, in this lonely atonement, Jesus "demonstrates his overwhelming desire to remain beyond his death and *forever the inseparable companion of every human being.*"[11]

How did such a lonely Messiah journey with others en route to the cross? Were friendships important to Jesus? Who were Jesus' friends, and how did Jesus decide who would receive an invitation to be his friend? Let us next consider what the Gospels reveal about the circle of friends that surrounded Jesus.

CHAPTER 2

Jesus' Circle of Friends

"No one has greater love than this,
to lay down one's life for one's friends.
You are my friends if you do what I command you."
—John 15:13-14

In *The Time of the Uprooted*, the great Jewish sage Elie Wiesel tells the story of Gamaliel, a Czech Jew who escaped to Hungary as a child during the Holocaust and survived under the care of a Christian woman. Years afterward, living in New York City, Gamaliel assesses the significance of the relationships that have shaped his life. Looking back, he paints a complicated and paradoxical picture:

> I think of the men and women whose paths have crossed my own. Some of them showed me the mystery of knowledge, others that of suffering. Whether they carried light or darkness, whether they were drawn to the service of good or attracted by evil, they all left their mark on me. It is because of them that I am who I am.[1]

As Jesus spent his last week in Jerusalem before his death, I imagine he also reflected on all the people whose paths had crossed with his. He had touched many lives through healings, exorcisms, lessons, and parables—and, likewise, he had been touched by others.

His love for the economically poor and the poor in spirit, for the lepers and the lost, for the widows and the children, for tax collectors and soldiers, and for both Jews and Samaritans, had propelled him toward Jerusalem and compelled him to embrace his sacrificial death. He was who he was—the Messiah of Israel and the Savior of the Gentiles—because of them.

The Paradox of Jesus' Loneliness and Friendship

Over the course of his earthly ministry, Jesus encountered a wonderful variety of people. Pharisees, Levites, priests and teachers of the Jewish law, shepherds, farmers, politicians, prostitutes, zealots, fishermen, day laborers, and kin crossed his path with regularity. Of these, some were rivals, some were enemies, some were passing acquaintances, and some were disciples and followers who spent virtually every day with him. But did Jesus have friends?

Few of us ever think to ask this question, and when we do, we encounter a vexing paradox that runs throughout Jesus' life. Jesus enters human history as Emmanuel—"God is with us" (Matthew 1:23). On a human level, his friendship circles are nicely filled; in this regard, he rightly serves as a role model. But because Jesus is also divine, there exists a gap between what is in his heart and what he can reveal to others; they can never fully understand him. Furthermore, Jesus' journey demands this paradox—as the suffering Messiah, Jesus must identify with sinful humanity and also be the scapegoat set apart for sacrifice. Thus, the paradox of friendship and loneliness is an essential feature of Jesus' mission journey. Consider these examples:

- Jesus spends three years walking among the masses, but sees through their adulation and does not let them get close to him (John 2:24).
- Jesus loves his family, but during his ministry, he is estranged from them. He fights with his mother during the wedding at Cana

(John 2:3-4) and seemingly snubs his family when they come to see him (see Matthew 12:46-50). He cannot perform miracles in his hometown because of their lack of faith in him (Mark 6:1-6).

- Jesus lodges in the homes of friends (like Lazarus), but proclaims, "Foxes have holes, and birds of the air have nests; but the Son of Man has nowhere to lay his head" (Matthew 8:20).

Jesus experienced some degree of isolation because others misunderstood his role. The masses yearned for a political rather than a spiritual Messiah, and in the end abandoned Jesus despite their initial enthusiasm for him. Jesus was estranged from his own family because of their opposition to his ministry—they actually tried to stop him: "When his family heard it, they went out to restrain him, for people were saying, 'He has gone out of his mind'" (Mark 3:21). Jesus' closest followers could not comprehend that his journey would lead to the cross (Luke 9:45; 18:34; John 10:6; 13:7; 20:39). Shusaku Endo, one of the greatest Japanese novelists of the twentieth century, observes, "Even while Jesus stood in the circle of his own disciples, he was alone."[2]

Endo's *A Life of Jesus* is not strictly a biography, but rather a reconstruction of Jesus' journey utilizing a novelist's imaginative skills. Endo revels in the paradox of Jesus' loneliness and isolation on the one hand, and Jesus' solidarity and presence with the "misfortunate" on the other. Jesus understood that the misfortunate were suffering for reasons that extended beyond their economic deprivation or physical pain: "Jesus knew that poverty and disease in themselves are not the hardest things to bear; the hardest to bear are the loneliness and the hopelessness that comes with being sick or poor."[3]

Endo's portrait affirms that Jesus, understanding humanity's need to overcome loneliness and isolation, enters our lives to provide a solution: "Jesus knew the longing of human beings for changeless, enduring companionship."[4] Paradoxically, Jesus provides us with just this kind of companionship by leaving us through an amazing display of love on the cross.

On the other side of Calvary, Jesus resumes his ministry of companionship as he encounters the forlorn disciples traveling to Emmaus (Luke 24:13-35). "What emerges clearly in that evening's touching story is the image of Jesus as companion," Endo observes.[5] And of course, in his final human words to the disciples, Jesus tells his friends, "And remember, I am with you always, to the end of the age" (Matthew 28:20). Now resurrected from the dead, Jesus is the Christian's eternal companion—and friend!

Jesus Reflects on Love, Friendship, and Mission

Even a cursory reading of the four Gospels reveals that Matthew, Mark, and Luke portray the story of Jesus' journey in a different way than John does. The three synoptic Gospels concentrate on the milestones of Jesus' public ministry. They speak of his birth, baptism, miracles, teachings, and travels. At the end of Jesus' life, they focus on Palm Sunday, the Last Supper, and Jesus' death and resurrection.

In contrast, the Gospel of John provides us with an account of Jesus' life that is both more intimate and more spiritual. In this Gospel attributed to the disciple "whom Jesus loved" (John 13:23), we see Jesus sharing with his friends in a way that is not seen in the other Gospels. Most significantly, five chapters of John's Gospel are devoted to Jesus' final teachings reserved for just his closest disciples. In John 13–17, Jesus shares insights and teachings that have been cherished by generations of Christians. John, Jesus' best friend, recognized that these conversations were important to preserve—and in doing so John demonstrates the sensitivity we would expect from the closest of friends. In this section, we encounter a very personal Jesus who is vulnerable, eager to reveal what is on his heart, and open to sharing the wisdom of his journey with those whom he loves.

What does Jesus share with his closest companions just before leaving them? With his days of performing public miracles and teaching thousands throughout Judea and Samaria completed, Jesus turns his attention to the culmination of his spiritual journey: the cross. We can only imagine Jesus' state of mind as he steels himself for Calvary. He seems to focus his heart and mind on his objective, and he wants his closest disciples and companions to understand the significance of what is coming. Throughout John 13–17, Jesus exposes his inner thoughts and feelings to his disciples on a range of issues—and the heart of this revelation is John 15.

After washing his disciples' feet to demonstrate how we follow God in humility (John 13), and comforting them by reiterating his promise that they could gain eternal life through him (John 14), Jesus declares that he is the true vine through which the kingdom of God is made manifest (15:1-8). He uses that metaphor of the vine and its branches to consider three key journey themes: *love, friendship,* and *mission.*

Most of us are more than able to give a common-sense definition of each of those terms. We know what we mean when we speak of love, of friendship, and of mission. And yet, as Jesus talks about these three aspects of his spiritual journey, it is as if they mystically merge into a greater whole. The lines between the three blur, and Jesus' understanding of each term depends upon the other two:

- Jesus defines *love* as giving one's life for one's friends (John 15:13).
- Jesus defines *friendship* in terms of following his command to love one another as he has loved us (15:9-10,12,17).
- Jesus defines *mission* as living fruitful lives that reflect our loving connection to Jesus and our God in heaven (15:8-10,15-16).

Love, friendship, and mission are three aspects of the beauty of the cross. And in the climax of Jesus' earthly journey, the three are merged in a single reality. This mirrors Christianity's understanding of the Trinity. Christians affirm a monotheistic notion of God—there is only one God, the God of Israel. Yet this God is revealed to us in three persons—traditionally named Father, Son, and Holy Spirit. The paradox of Christian Trinitarian theology is that the one God is a *complex unity*.

In like manner, love, friendship, and mission each fully represent the spiritual reality of the cross. It is as if Jesus is offering us a formula: *Love x Friendship x Mission = Calvary.* Love is fully expressed through the cross; friendship is fully epitomized by the cross; and God's mission is fulfilled perfectly in the cross.

When we contemplate the spiritual significance of the atonement, friendship is rarely given its due. We don't tend to think of friendship as one of the essentials of Christian theology. Yet at this most pivotal moment in Jesus' life, in his last words to his disciples before he would go to the cross, Jesus chooses to highlight the theme of friendship. These teachings, spoken in the company of many of Jesus' dearest friends, indicate that friendship is an essential aspect of the kingdom of God. Friendship is not a secondary issue, but a core concern for all who seek to follow Jesus and to take up our crosses daily.

Why is friendship so important to Jesus? What does God want us to learn from Jesus' example?

First, *friendship embodies sacrificial love.* "No one has greater love than this, to lay down one's life for one's friends" (John 15:13). Our willingness to give of ourselves for others is a measure of our friendship with them.

Second, *friendship expresses the covenantal relationship we have with Christ and others in God's kingdom.* "You are my friends if you do what I command you" (John 15:14). Between friends, obedience does not take the form of legalistic adherence to rules, but is instead expressed through joyful actions done on behalf of another. In relationships, obedience is an effort to *please* the other person. We follow Christ's commands out of gratitude for what God has done for us, and we are motivated to obey by love. Paul and John reiterate this principle many times in their letters:

- "Live as children of light—for the fruit of the light is found in all that is good and right and true. Try to find out what is pleasing to the Lord" (Ephesians 5:8-10).
- "...lead lives worthy of the Lord, fully pleasing to him, as you bear fruit in every good work and as you grow in the knowledge of God" (Colossians 1:10).
- "...we speak, not to please mortals, but to please God who tests our hearts" (1 Thessalonians 2:4).
- "Beloved, if our hearts do not condemn us, we have boldness before God; and we receive from him whatever we ask, because we obey his commandments and do what pleases him" (1 John 3:21-22).

Third, *friendship involves self-revelation—sharing the secrets of our souls.* "I have called you friends, because I have made known to you everything that I have heard from my Father" (John 15:15). Friends reveal their hearts to us and are willing to receive our secrets with appreciation and acceptance. Looking forward to the friendship of heaven, Paul states, "For now we see in a mirror, dimly, but then we will see face to face. Now I know only in part; then I will know fully, even as I have been fully known" (1 Corinthians 13:12).

Fourth, *friendship is a choice.* "You did not choose me but I chose you. And I appointed you to go and bear fruit, fruit that will last..." (John 15:16). In God's kingdom, choosing our friends involves not only the desire to enter into personal relationships with these people, but also to fulfill God's will within these relationships by bearing fruit.

This understanding of the spiritual purpose of friendship is not unlike the new definition of *family* Jesus offers when his biological family seeks him out:

> Then his mother and his brothers came; and standing outside, they sent to him and called him. A crowd was sitting around him; and they said to him, "Your mother and your brothers and sisters are outside, asking for you." And he replied, "Who are my mother and my brothers?" And looking at those who sat around him, he said, "Here are my mother and my brothers! Whoever does the will of God is my brother and sister and mother." (Mark 3:31-35; see also Matthew 12:46-50)

Jesus' use of "brother and sister" in this story is analogous to his definition of "friend" in John 15. This is even clearer in Luke's version of the account, where Jesus says, "My mother and my brothers are those who hear the word of God and do it" (Luke 8:21). We may not get to choose our biological family, but we do choose those with whom we journey as we seek to follow God.

Jesus and His Circles of Friends

God loves the whole world and every person in it, but Jesus does not invite everyone he meets to become a personal friend. Like us, Jesus experiences the full range of human relationships. Some people love to be with Jesus, others are indifferent to him, and some view him as an enemy. Jesus goes out of his way to spend his free time with some people, while others receive less of his time and attention.

Who are Jesus' friends? Let's exercise our imaginations and attempt to reconstruct the web of relationships Jesus enjoyed as an adult. At the outset, we must recognize that our source materials—the four Gospels—were not written with this question in mind, so they do not provide all the information we'd need to be sure our reconstruction is totally accurate. Furthermore, the data we have is sometimes ambiguous or sketchy; it is quite possible you may not agree with all my conclusions.

As we seek to create a snapshot of Jesus' friendships, it's worth noting that friendships are not static. Friends come and go as time passes. To create the most accurate picture of Jesus' friendships, we must pick a date. I've chosen Palm Sunday—five days before Jesus dies. Of course, we could choose any date in Jesus' life, but more information is available if we seek to illustrate Jesus' relationships on a date toward the end of Jesus' journey.

On Palm Sunday, there were people whom Jesus had alienated or found himself at odds with. Many Pharisees and legal scholars were disillusioned with Jesus before he entered Jerusalem (Luke 11:53-54). With just a few notable exceptions (including Nicodemus and Joseph of Arimathea), as an adult Jesus did not draw many friends from these groups.

Jesus had many acquaintances—people he met once (such as the woman at the well or the dozens of people he prayed for and healed), but these people could hardly be called friends. They knew his name, and he may have known theirs—but there was no ongoing sharing of life together.

There were some people who'd had important relationships with Jesus earlier in his life, but who were no longer engaged in an active friendship with him. His father, Joseph, is not mentioned in any of the Gospels as playing any role in Jesus' adult life; scholars assume Joseph passed away before Jesus reached full adulthood. Similarly, John the Baptist died early in Jesus' ministry period. As relatives, John and Jesus most likely enjoyed a childhood friendship, and Jesus' affection for him is demonstrated in his testimony concerning John's place in the kingdom of God (Luke 7:24-28).

The place of Jesus' mother, Mary, within his friendship circles is open to much debate and speculation. During Jesus' childhood and into early adulthood, they probably were very close. According to Jewish tradition, as the firstborn son in a family where the father has died, Jesus had a special responsibility to assist Mary in caring for the needs of the family. There are hints of a rift in the relationship as Jesus begins his public ministry—for example, at the wedding in Cana (see John 2:4), and of course, when Mary and the rest of the family seem to think Jesus had gone insane (Mark 3:21)! To a large extent, Jesus seems to prefer the company of his new family of disciples (Mark 3:31-35); yet Mary is generally counted to be among his most faithful followers (see John 19:25-27).[6]

Jesus had relationships of varying significance with both men and women. In addition to the Twelve, there were many other dedicated followers of Jesus (see Acts 1:15, where Peter speaks to a crowd of 120 believers who'd been with Jesus prior to his ascension). In addition to men like Joseph of Arimathea, who buried Jesus' body (Luke 23:50-53), Jesus inspired the loyal (and financial) support of a group of women, some of whom Luke mentions by name:

> Soon afterwards he went on through cities and villages, proclaiming and bringing the good news of the kingdom of God. The twelve were with him, as well as some women who had been cured of evil spirits and infirmities: Mary, called Magdalene, from whom seven demons had gone out, and Joanna, the wife of Herod's steward Chuza, and Susanna, and many others, who provided for them out of their resources. (Luke 8:1-3; see also Luke 23:49-56; Acts 1:14)

We see all the signs of genuine friendship between Jesus and his band of twelve disciples. They traveled, worked, and ate together regularly for some three years. Perhaps he'd known some of them before they were called to join his group. And it's not hard to discern differing levels of closeness between Jesus and the twelve men. Peter, James, and John stand out from the others. Jesus takes them with him at key milestone experiences in his journey, such as the

Mount of Transfiguration glorification (Matthew 17:1-13) and Gethsemane (Matthew 26:36-46). And of these three, only John is called "the one whom Jesus loved" (John 13:23; 20:2). There are even indications of rivalry between Peter and John embedded in the Gospels (see John 20:1-9, where John outruns Peter to the empty tomb; and John 21:15-24, where Peter inquires inappropriately about John's future).

In addition to the twelve apostles, there was one family of three that seemed to be particularly close to Jesus. Siblings Martha, Mary, and Lazarus all clearly enjoyed a deep friendship with Jesus; John declares, "Jesus loved Martha and her sister and Lazarus" (John 11:5). They loved him as well, even to the point of sibling rivalry for his attention and affection (see Luke 10:38-42). Martha (who was probably the older sister) demonstrated her affection by serving in a traditional first-century woman's role and resented that Mary took the liberty of sitting at Jesus' feet and listening to him when there was work to be done. Jesus, in affirming Mary's choice indicates the degree to which he welcomed an intimate and equal friendship with the sisters as well as their brother.

The closeness of the relationship between Jesus and this family is also affirmed in Lazarus's resurrection story. Although only recorded in John's Gospel, the narrative represents a critical juncture in the journey of Jesus. It is the final public miracle, and a foreshadowing of Jesus' own resurrection (John 11:1-44). Jesus saved his last miraculous sign for one of his closest friends.

In this interaction, Martha goes out to meet Jesus while Mary stays behind at home. When Martha challenges Jesus with the confidence of a close friend—"Lord, if you had been here, my brother would not have died" (John 11:21)—he responds with compassion and assurance. But Jesus also notices Mary's absence and sends Martha back with a message: "The Teacher is here, and is calling for you" (John 11:28). Mary responds by rushing to meet him:

> When Mary came where Jesus was and saw him, she knelt at his feet and said to him, "Lord, if you had been here, my brother would not have died." When Jesus saw her weeping, and the Jews who came with her also weeping, he was greatly disturbed in spirit and deeply moved. He said, "Where have you laid him?" They said to him, "Lord, come and see." Jesus began to weep. So the Jews said, "See how he loved him!" (John 11:32-36)

Mary's tears moved and troubled Jesus even before he faced Lazarus's tomb. And why not? When a close friend is troubled, one's heart is troubled too. Mary's ability to evoke Jesus' tears—and his ability to evoke hers (see John 12:1-8; also 11:1-2)—testify to the deep love and intimate friendship they shared.

A Picture of the Friendship Circles of Jesus

Using the *Friendship Circles* model (see the following page for Figure 1), it is possible to imagine Jesus' web of relationships by placing his friends within a set of concentric circles. (We'll talk about the model in more detail later in the book. For now, we simply need to understand that each circle represents a different level of relationship, with Jesus' closer friends nearer the bull's-eye.) On Palm Sunday, a picture of Jesus' friendship circles at the culmination of his earthly ministry might look like the Figure on the following page.

As I've sketched them, Jesus' friendship circles have a sense of balance. In the innermost circle, John and Mary symbolize God's friendship with men and women. The second circle shows a combination of work and non-work friendships. The third circle adds variety to Jesus' web of relationships, but also hints at loss. (John the Baptist might have been in this circle if he had survived. Judas will soon depart from Jesus' circle of friends because of his betrayal.) The outermost circle recognizes that Jesus had other significant family and non-family relationships.

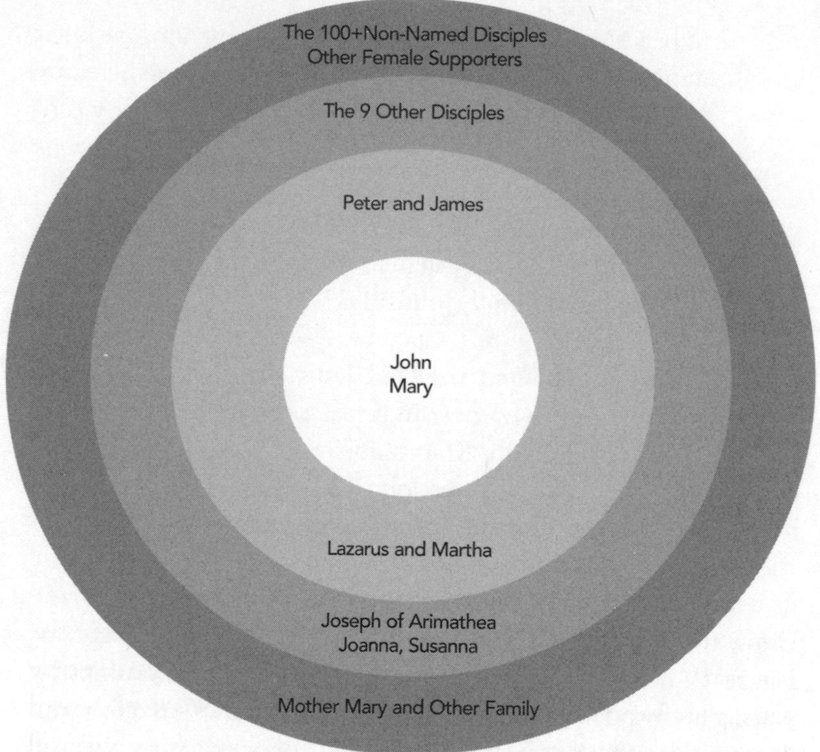

Figure 1: Jesus' Circles of Friendship on Palm Sunday

Jesus' friendship circle choices are full enough to satisfy his need and desire for connection with others, yet selective enough to permit him to pay an appropriate amount of attention to each friend. Both women and men are well represented. Each friend had a role to play in furthering Jesus' spiritual journey; even those who were not faithful (see John 6:60-66).

Jesus expressed and lived out his Messianic call in and through his friendships, and through the stories of his friends. He now calls out to each of us with an offer of his friendship—and an invitation to share that friendship with others.

CHAPTER 3

Friendship in the Bible

"Thus the LORD used to speak to Moses face to face,
as one speaks to a friend."
—Exodus 33:11

The Bible does not offer a systematic treatment of the subject of friendship, even though descriptions of all kinds of friendships fill its pages. The biblical writers appear to accept the reality of friendship in the same way they accept the existence of the atmosphere. It is just "there" and all around us, and they assume that people will naturally appreciate great friendships when they are presented as part of the historical and theological unfolding of God's will through Israel in the Old Testament and the church in the New Testament. Aside from some scattered Proverbs concerning how to conduct our friendships and their importance to us, the Bible gives very little direct advice regarding how to embrace new friends, maintain those relationships, and expand the circle of our friends.

Of course, much of the counsel found in the wisdom literature of the Old Testament and in the letters of the New Testament can be applied to our relationships with our friends. In chapter two, I highlighted the connection between Jesus' messianic journey and his friendships. In this chapter, I shall tie the Scriptures' descriptions of friendship to the general narrative of salvation history. I believe this to be the best methodology for creating a theology of friendship.

The Genesis of Friendship: Friendship with God

The two most significant friendships described in the Old Testament are the relationships that both Abraham and Moses enjoyed not with other humans, but with God. Although Abraham and Moses were not the first people God attempted to befriend, their friendships with God provide the foundation for Israel to live as a covenant people, and they serve as inspirational examples for all who wish to journey as friends of God.

Prior to Abraham, God's friendship with Adam and Eve (Genesis 1–3) was destroyed by their disobedience to God's command. Their fall from friendship came in two steps. They disobeyed God by eating from the tree of the knowledge of good and evil. However, even before their fall, they did not perform a positive act that would have guaranteed their friendship with God for eternity; they did not eat from the tree of life. Their lack of faith in God's covenantal friendship led to a weakening of their friendship with their Creator. The demise of their spiritual friendship with God introduced alienation and death into the world.

Generations later, Enoch sought and received God's friendship, and saw a reversal of Adam and Eve's curse (death). Like Noah in a later time (Genesis 6:9), Enoch "walked with God" (see Genesis 5:21-25). This deceptively pedestrian phrase indicates that Enoch embraced and fulfilled God's will in his spiritual journeys, and that he enjoyed a personal friendship—an ongoing relationship—with God. Echoing Paul, the writer to the Hebrews says of Enoch: "By faith Enoch was taken so that he did not experience death; and 'he was not found, because God had taken him.' For it was attested before he was taken away that 'he had *pleased* God'" (Hebrews 11:5; emphasis mine). Pleasing one's friends is the essence of friendship, and it is intimately connected to fulfilling God's will in our journeys.

Abraham epitomizes the perspective on friendship found throughout Genesis: The key imperative of life is to journey with

God as God's friend. King Jehoshaphat may have been the first Jewish leader to cite Abraham as God's friend (2 Chronicles 20:7). A century later, Isaiah will do the same (Isaiah 41:8), and the New Testament confirms the designation: "'Abraham believed God, and it was reckoned to him as righteousness,' and he was called the friend of God" (James 2:23). Abraham is God's friend because he journeys by faith toward the goal God reveals and because he maintains an ongoing personal relationship with God all along the way. The Genesis description of Abraham's dealings with God encompasses all of the earmarks of authentic friendship (Genesis 12–25):

- God and Abraham express covenantal loyalty and fidelity to each other. (Genesis 12:1-3; 15:1-21; 17:1-27)
- They act in cooperation with each other. (Genesis 20:17-18; 24:1-9)
- They converse on a regular basis. (Genesis 12:1-3; 13:14-17; 15:1-6; 17:1-27; 18:1-33)
- They reveal their plans, dreams, and fears. (Genesis 17:1-27; 18:17)
- They debate, bargain with, and prod each other. (Genesis 18:16-33)
- Each of them takes the other's feelings into consideration. (Genesis 15:1-21)
- They are willing to sacrifice for each other. (Genesis 22:1-19)

Abraham surely enjoyed friendships with other people, but Genesis focuses on his relationship with God. The same can be said of the presentation of Moses' friendships, as described in Exodus, Numbers, Leviticus, and Deuteronomy. Moses may have valued his friendships with Jethro and Joshua, but his friendship with God demands center stage. What greater compliment could ever be proffered than this: "Thus the LORD used to speak to Moses face to face, as one speaks to a friend" (Exodus 33:11)? All the features of friendship that Abraham enjoyed with God are also found in

Moses' relationship with God. The unmediated conversations Abraham and Moses had with God, coupled with their faithfulness in journeying in response to God's command, constitute the two essential pillars of spiritual friendship.

Centuries later, Joel's prophecy would offer to all God's people the possibility of having the same kind of friendship with God that Abraham and Moses enjoyed. Joel foresees a day when God's people will converse with God through dreams and visions, and have access to God in a way that previously had been restricted to prophets, kings, and priests (Joel 2:28-32). The Holy Spirit will anoint and empower God's friends so they can embrace and fulfill God's call to mission (see Acts 2:1-41). The Old Testament's conception of friendship with God sets the stage for the church's experience of friendship with God through Jesus.

Naomi, Orpah, and Ruth: Intergenerational and Cross-cultural Friendships

The period of the Judges was a time of political chaos and social dislocation in Israel. The book of Ruth chronicles the story of one Jewish family during that period. Elimelech and Naomi, with their two sons, leave Bethlehem during a food shortage and resettle in Moab. The sons marry Moabite women (Orpah and Ruth), and then calamity strikes—all three men in the family die (Ruth 1:1-5). Naomi decides to return to Bethlehem and gives her two daughters by marriage the option of staying in Moab. Both initially say they will go along, but ultimately only Ruth undertakes the journey with Naomi (Ruth 1:6-19).

Traditionally, most readers have celebrated Ruth's choice to travel with her mother-in-law and are critical of Orpah's decision to remain in her home country. But we should not be so quick to cast Orpah in a negative light. Cynthia Ozick, a contemporary Jewish novelist and distinguished literary essayist, provides a wonderfully positive appraisal of Orpah:

> Orpah has cut through all this bad blood [between Israel and Moab] to plain humanity; it would be unfair to consider her inferior to any other kindhearted young woman who ever lived in the world before or ever since. She is in fact superior; she has thrown off prejudice, and she has had to endure more than most young women of her class, including the less spunky and the less amiable: an early widowhood and no babies.[1]

Prodded by Ozick's resuscitation of Orpah's reputation and status in the story, I wish to offer a reinterpretation of the journey of these three women. Setting aside traditional understandings which focus on the story as an explanation of how the Messiah comes through David's familial line (an important theme, to be sure!), let's appreciate the story for its insights into friendship.

The relationships among the three women offer a positive and sophisticated affirmation of friendships. They treat one another with affection, love, respect, and courtesy. They support and assist one another through tragedy. Freedom of choice is granted, and even when there is a parting of the ways, it is accomplished amicably.

These friendships also cross significant boundaries. The relationships are both intergenerational and cross-cultural. It also is a friendship that crosses religious boundaries. The friendship between Naomi and Ruth is close enough to encourage the younger woman to embrace Naomi's faith: "Where you go, I will go…your people shall be my people, and your God my God" (Ruth 1:16).

The friendship of Naomi, Orpah, and Ruth may be appreciated from a spiritual journey perspective. Friendships are not always meant to be life-long; changes in circumstances naturally lead to the ending of some relationships. Naomi's decision to move back to her homeland signified just such an occasion for Orpah, who as a Moabite had no natural motivation to move to a foreign country. Ruth felt differently, and decided to continue the journey link between her life and Naomi's. Her dedication to make the friendship lifelong (Ruth 1:17) is as admirable as it was risky.

The friendship between Naomi and Ruth changed the course of Hebrew history and Jewish religion. While recalling a childhood memory of two portraits on her wall (one of her Jewish grandfather and the other of a picture she interprets as being of Ruth), Ozick observes:

> The Book of Ruth—wherein goodness grows out of goodness, and the extraordinary is found here, and here, and here—is sown in desertion, bereavement, barrenness, death, loss, displacement, destitution. What can sprout from such ash? Then Ruth sees into the nature of Covenant, and the life of the story streams in. Out of this stalk mercy and redemption unfold; flowers flood Ruth's feet; and my grandfather goes on following her track until the coming of the Messiah from the shoot of David, in the line of Ruth and Naomi.[2]

Or, said another way, we all owe the coming of the Messiah to the friendship of these women.

David, Jonathan, and Saul: Loyalty, Love, Ambition, and Friendship

The biblical accounts of the life of David name a number of people as his friends, including "the elders of Judah" (1 Samuel 30:26) and Hushai (2 Samuel 15:37; 16:16). But one friendship stands out above all others—David's relationship with Jonathan: "When David had finished speaking to Saul, the soul of Jonathan was bound to the soul of David, and Jonathan loved him as his own soul...Then Jonathan made a covenant with David, because he loved him as his own soul" (1 Samuel 18:1-3).

The covenant between David and Jonathan holds through various trials. Even though Jonathan has a valid claim to succeed his father, Saul, as ruler of Israel, he recognizes that God has called David to be king. Accordingly, he does not allow his father's paranoid actions to create a wedge between him and his closest friend. Jonathan sacrifices ambition for friendship (1 Samuel 19:1-7).

David returns the favor. David mourns Jonathan with the words: "Greatly beloved were you to me; your love to me was wonderful, passing the love of women" (2 Samuel 1:26). David later fulfills his vow to demonstrate loving-kindness or *hesed*—the key Hebrew term for covenant loyalty, often translated as faithfulness, mercy, or steadfast love—to Jonathan's family by accepting Jonathan's surviving son, Mephibosheth, as a regular guest at the royal table (see 1 Samuel 20:14-16; 2 Samuel 9:1-13).

Of course, David's relationship with Saul is not as harmonious as his friendship with Jonathan. There are times when the two strong-willed men are able to get along (1 Samuel 19:7). David's musical skills on the harp often comfort Saul's bedeviled soul (see 1 Samuel 16:16-23). Most of the time, though, Saul's jealousy prevents him from enjoying a true friendship with David. However, David refuses, on two different occasions, to act on opportunities to harm Saul because it would have been a sign of rebellion and dishonor against the anointed and acknowledged leader of God's people (1 Samuel 24:1-15; 26:1-25). Later, when David learns of Saul's death, he seems to be genuinely saddened by Saul's demise (2 Samuel 1:11-27). We can only wonder what kind of relationship might have been realized between these two men if Saul had followed the example of his own son. Ambition should never be allowed to trump friendship.

Job and His Friends: The Search for Consolation

How do we comfort a friend who is suffering from a crisis of faith or a devastating loss? When Job's three friends hear about his calamity, they visit him in order to "console and comfort him"

(Job 2:11). For a week, they share Job's pain by weeping, tearing their clothes in mourning, and by maintaining respectful silence (2:12-13). What a great way to demonstrate their friendship! Sensing support and love, Job expresses his feelings of grief and torment (3:1-26). Up to this point, Job's friends have related to him well.

However, beginning with Eliphaz's first reply (Job 4), they falter in their mission. Mistaking Job's questions and railings against God as evidence of heretofore hidden impiety and self-righteousness, they try to convince Job he deserves the punishment that has befallen him. The more Job defends himself, the more they withdraw their initial support and love, and become, in effect, his accusers instead of his comforters.

C.G. Jung, in what amounts to a diatribe against the God of the Bible in light of Job's crisis, pauses for just one moment to aim his fire at Job's human friends: "Job's friends do everything in their power to contribute to his moral torments, and instead of giving him, whom God has perfidiously abandoned, their warm-hearted support, they moralize in an all too human manner, that is, in the stupidest fashion imaginable, and 'fill him with wrinkles.'"[3]

In the midst of his crisis, Job is not looking to his friends for answers, but rather for acceptance and emotional support. He cries, "A despairing man should have the devotion of his friends" (Job 6:14, NIV; see also 19:13-22). Later in the story, a fourth friend, Elihu, errs similarly by trying to set Job straight (Job 32–37). Consolation is all Job asks for, but those who come to listen to him have ceased to hear his pained soul.

The point is clear: Friends best serve one another as comforters. Advice should be offered prudently, and we should not seek to force a friend to resolve a crisis by offering counsel when our perspective is limited. Only God can effect the transformation needed to pull a person out of the depths of spiritual doubt and despair. A friend experiencing a spiritual crisis usually does not need our theological correctives but rather our supportive presence and love, so that he or she does not have to live out the crisis in isolation.

At the end of Job's story, God directly intervenes and brings Job's crisis to a positive and deeply transformational conclusion. To our ears, the series of questions God poses to Job in chapters 38–41 may seem as judgmental as the advice of his four friends, but I prefer to see them as a sign of God's friendship with Job. The questions, both individually and as a set, are designed to elevate Job's sight, to bring forth awe and wonder, and to help Job realize the vastness and great mystery of the universe—and of God's purposes within it. Humbled, Job emerges from his encounter with God a more spiritual person: "My ears had heard of you but now my eyes have seen you" (Job 42:5). Job does not receive support from his peers, but in the end he does find wisdom through his friendship with God.

The Wisdom of Proverbs: Journeying with the Right Friends

The writers of Proverbs prudently urge us to exercise due diligence and caution in choosing our friends, because they will exert significant influence over our spiritual journeys: "The righteous gives good advice to friends, but the way of the wicked leads astray" (Proverbs 12:26). Good friends can help us in difficult situations: "A friend loves at all times, and kinsfolk are born to share adversity" (Proverbs 17:17; see also Ecclesiastes 4:10). However, other relationships may have a negative impact on our lives: "Make no friends with those given to anger, and do not associate with hotheads, or you may learn their ways and entangle yourself in a snare" (Proverbs 22:24-25). Evil people are to be avoided at all costs, no matter how intriguing their invitations may be:

> My child, if sinners entice you, do not consent. If they say, "Come with us, let us lie in wait for blood; let us wantonly ambush the innocent; like Sheol let us swallow them alive and whole, like those who go down to the Pit. We shall find all kinds of costly things; we shall fill our houses with booty. Throw in your lot among us; we will all have one purse"—my child, do not walk in their way, keep your foot from their paths; for their feet run to evil, and they hurry to shed blood. (Proverbs 1:10-16; see also 4:10-17)

The Prophets' Lament: The Demise of Friendship

In the eyes of the prophets, friendship falls on hard times! Israel and Judah, in forsaking friendship with God by failing to adhere to the values of the Mosaic Covenant, reap the fruit of their spiritual rebellion in all spheres of life. Individual immorality, religious idolatry, and social injustice lead to God's judgment and exile. Listen to the words of the prophets:

- Learn to do good; seek justice, rescue the oppressed, defend the orphan, plead for the widow. Come now, let us argue it out, says the LORD (Isaiah 1:17-18).
- Have you not just now called to me, "My Father, you are the friend of my youth—will he be angry forever, will he be indignant to the end?" (Jeremiah 3:4-5).
- Therefore thus says the LORD: "See, I am laying before this people stumbling blocks against which they shall stumble; parents and children together, neighbor and friend shall perish" (Jeremiah 6:21).
- Beware of your friends; do not trust your brothers. For every brother is a deceiver, and every friend a slanderer. Friend deceives friend, and no one speaks the truth (Jeremiah 9:4-5, NIV).

■ Put no trust in a friend, have no confidence in a loved one (Micah 7:5).

The verdict of the Old Testament prophets is clear: Friendship has failed. Can it ever be revived?

Jesus' New Covenant: The Revival of Friendship

We considered Jesus' personal friendships in chapter 2, knowing that his interactions often speak more loudly than words. But Jesus did spend a lot of his time among us teaching, so let us also consider his words for insights about how we are called to relate to (and befriend) one another.

Jesus demonstrates (through healings and miracles) and proclaims (through parables and lessons) the coming of the kingdom of God: "Jesus went throughout Galilee, teaching in their synagogues and proclaiming the good news of the kingdom and curing every disease and every sickness among the people" (Matthew 4:23; see also 4:17). Manifesting the kingdom of God is the goal of the New Covenant, which was anticipated by the prophets as they watched the demise of faithful friendship in relation to both God and others (Jeremiah 31; Ezekiel 36-37). Jesus' vision for the kingdom of God is expressed most fully in the Sermon on the Mount (Matthew 5–7; see also Luke 6).

The Sermon on the Mount outlines Jesus' expectations for how his disciples should relate to others; thus it serves as his call for the revival of authentic covenantal friendship with both God and other people. We are to be both "salt" and "light" by modeling God's righteousness in such a way that others may be led into Christ's grace (Matthew 5:13-16). Jesus calls us to relate to people on a high ethical and moral plane, recognizing that righteousness of the heart demands higher standards and a deeper sense of obedience to God than can be gained from a superficial or legalistic conformity to God's commandments (5:17-20). Hate is likened to murder; lust is equated with adultery. Justice must embrace compassion, and love must be expressed to one's enemies as well as one's friends (5:21-48). The spiritual disciplines of charity, prayer, and fasting should be practiced in secrecy so that improper motives will not corrupt our relationships with God and others (6:1-18).

Our earthly activities should be viewed from a heavenly perspective. Serving God must take priority over a life of materialism because God will provide for the needs of those who "strive first for the kingdom of God and his righteousness" (6:19-34). Our judgments of other people's failings must always be tempered by remembering our own unfaithfulness and sinfulness (7:1-6). The Golden Rule is an apt summary of the relational perspective of the Sermon on the Mount: "In everything do to others as you would have them do to you; for this is the law and the prophets" (7:12). The kingdom of God, in both its Old and New Covenant incarnations, calls us to accept God's friendship and extend such friendship to others.[4]

The Church of Jesus: A Community Where Friendship Reigns

Jesus' death and resurrection are God's most profound demonstration of friendship as well as friendship's ultimate vindication. In response, the apostles immediately create a community of spiritual friendship that seeks to exemplify the relational vision of the Sermon on the Mount:

> They devoted themselves to the apostles' teaching and fellowship, to the breaking of bread and the prayers. Awe came upon everyone, because many wonders and signs were being done by the apostles. All who believed were together and had all things in common; they would sell their possessions and goods and distribute the proceeds to all, as any had need. Day by day, as they spent much time together in the temple, they broke bread at home and ate their food with glad and generous hearts, praising God

> and having the goodwill of all the people… (Acts 2:42-47; see also 4:32-35)

Yet relations among these Christian friends are not always so ideal. The two great controversies in Acts—the distribution of food to Greek and Hebraic widows (Acts 6:1-4) and the entry of Gentiles into the church (Acts 15)—threaten to disrupt the unity of the community of Jesus' follower-friends. And challenges continue to confront the church as it expands throughout the Roman Empire. The letters from Paul, Peter, and John can all be read as appeals to maintain and deepen the friendships Christians enjoy in Christ. Among the many examples from Paul's letters are the great love appeal in 1 Corinthians 13, the unity appeal based on Jesus' journey in Philippians 2, and the fruit of the Spirit appeal in Galatians 5. Similarly, 1 John reads like a sermon based on Jesus' words about love, friendship, and mission recorded in John 15. Consider this familiar passage:

> Dear friends, let us love one another, for love comes from God. Everyone who loves has been born of God and knows God. Whoever does not love does not know God, because God is love. This is how God showed his love among us: He sent his one and only Son into the world that we might live through him. This is love: not that we loved God, but that he loved us and sent his Son as an atoning sacrifice for our sins. Dear friends, since God so loved us, we also ought to love one another. (1 John 4:7-11, NIV)

Friends Are Forever: Heaven, Marriage, and Friendship

In contemporary Western societies, we often pit marriage and friendship against one another. Many studies indicate that when a person develops a romantic relationship with a potential partner, he or she will tend to devote less time and attention to platonic relationships.

But Jesus is different. He remains celibate throughout his life and never marries. Even though both the Hebrew Scriptures and Jewish culture assume it is normative and good to marry and to have children, Jesus does not seek either for himself. Instead, as a "eunuch" for the kingdom of heaven (Matthew 19:12), he enters into a diverse array of friendships. When his theological adversaries challenge him to an arcane debate about the afterlife, Jesus unexpectedly asserts the superiority of friendship over marriage:

> "Those who belong to this age marry and are given in marriage; but those who are considered worthy of a place in that age and in the resurrection from the dead neither marry nor are given in marriage. Indeed they cannot die anymore, because they are like angels and are children of God, being children of the resurrection." (Luke 20:34-36; see also Matthew 22:30-32)

Jesus declares that marriage—the deepest sexual relationship for humans and a sacred symbol of the spiritual life—will be rendered obsolete in heaven. In Scripture, the relationship between God and God's people is likened to marriage: "Let us rejoice and exult and give him the glory, for the marriage of the Lamb has come, and his bride has made herself ready" (Revelation 19:7; see also Ezekiel 16; Hosea 1–3; Ephesians 5). We will not be married to other human beings in heaven because collectively, the people of God will be "married" (meaning fully united in complete love) to Jesus, their Messiah and Savior!

Jesus refers to himself as the bridegroom (Matthew 9:15; 25:1-10; Mark 2:19; Luke 5:34). But this lacks any sexual undertones, for marriage for Jesus seems to be just one more way to express his desire for eternal companionship, friendship, and sharing with those he redeems. On the Mount of Transfiguration, Jesus conducts a deep conversation with Moses and Elijah (Matthew 17:1-3). Is this a foreshadowing of the kind of relationship we all will have with Jesus when we are resurrected? Conversation is a key element of friendship! Being together is another; to the criminal on the cross beside him, Jesus says, "Truly I tell you, today you will be with me in Paradise" (Luke 23:43).

And then there is one of the greatest promises in all of Scripture, words spoken by Jesus just before the John 15 discourse on love, friendship, and mission:

> Do not let your hearts be troubled. Believe in God, believe also in me. In my Father's house there are many dwelling places. If it were not so, would I have told you that I go to prepare a place for you? And if I go and prepare a place for you, I will come again and will take you to myself, so that where I am, there you may be also." (John 14:1-3)

What are we to think, then, of human relationships in heaven? Since marriage is the symbol reserved for our relationship with God, another term needs to be found to define our relationship with one another in eternity. That term is *friendship*. In the post-resurrection perfection of heaven where sin is absent, human alienation, isolation, and insecurity will be replaced by the deepest kind of acceptance, vulnerability, faithfulness, loyalty, and love. Our sharing with one another will be deep, authentic, and filled with insight that only the perspective of eternity can provide.

CHAPTER 4

Seven Steps for Deepening Friendship

"...friendship is the springboard to every other love."
—Alan Loy McGinnis, *The Friendship Factor*[1]

Every church believes itself to be a welcoming and friendly fellowship, but this isn't always true. As a regional pastor, I travel to a different church almost every Sunday to preach or teach. One Sunday, I arrived early at a church that I was visiting for the first time. The facility was fairly large, and I decided to explore it and search for the pastor. Amazingly, once inside the building, I passed five people (presumably members of the church) as I wandered the halls—and not one of them took the initiative to acknowledge my presence by greeting me! I said hello to each person—but no one seemed to care enough to engage me in conversation. None of them asked who I was or why I was in the building. It wasn't quite the reception I anticipated, and certainly not one any visitor or prospective member should receive!

Most churches provide a friendlier environment than the one I just described. Volunteer greeters welcome visitors as they enter the building, and church members shake hands with newcomers during the greeting portion of the service. Some churches ask that visitors stand and introduce themselves, and some even prepare gifts for first-time guests. These gestures of friendliness are to be commended. But if our churches are to become spiritual communities where faithful friendship is expressed, we need to move beyond merely welcoming newcomers and one another. Friendliness is not friendship! This chapter offers a seven-step approach for deepening our understanding of friendship so that we may better appreciate its role in our personal lives and in our church families.

Step One: Recognize the Complex Nature of Friendship

Why do we find it difficult to define *friendship*? We all have a sense of what friendship is; yet most of us find it very tough to put words around it. Friendship is a universal relational experience that is expressed in differing ways through specific encounters within various cultures. It is a complex phenomenon. Furthermore, its parameters and possibilities change as we move through the various life stages.

Despite the difficulty, creating a personal definition of friendship is a worthwhile endeavor to undertake, because it has significant ramifications for how we use our time and for how we develop expectations for church life and ministry. To do this, we must recognize the complex realities and questions surrounding our own understanding of friendship. Consider how you'd answer each of these questions:

- How have I experienced friendship in my life?
- What kinds of friendship have I experienced and which ones have meant the most to me?
- How do I differentiate between close friendships and those that are more casual?
- How do the intensities of my feelings toward a friend correlate with that person's level of closeness to me?
- Can relatives be friends? Do all my relatives have to also be my friends?

■ Can lovers be friends? Must my spouse be my best friend?
■ How about my children—under what conditions can they be said to be friends?

With regard to church life, we might ask these additional questions:

■ Is it possible for me to be friends with everyone in my church? Why or why not?
■ How should I define my relationship with my pastor? Is she or he automatically a friend based on our pastoral relationship?
■ How do I remain open to making new friends when I have so little time to devote to my existing relationships?
■ What activities and gatherings in my church are friendship-friendly?

We may not agree on the answers to all these questions—and that is fine. The goal is not to develop a uniform definition of friendship we all must adopt, but rather to become aware of our own expectations, hopes, needs, and dreams.

Step Two: Appreciate the Dynamics of Friendship

The second step is to appreciate the dynamics of contemporary friendship. These include, but may not be limited to, the following seven principles of friendship:

1. *Although we may know many people by name, these individuals are not necessarily close or even casual friends.* They may be only acquaintances. Relatives, coworkers, schoolmates, mentors, fellow hobbyists, neighbors, and people we serve in ministry may be friends—but do not necessarily have to be.

2. *Over time, friends may grow closer to us or drift away.* This is a natural part of every person's journey. Some friendships may

last a lifetime, while others are meant to thrive for just a period of our lives.

3. *There is no "right" or normative number of friends we should have at any given time in our lives.* Many factors (such as culture, health, vocational transitions, marriage, births, or deaths) will impact the number and quality of friendships we experience and maintain. (For example, it is more difficult to accept invitations to socialize when we have infants or young children.)

4. *Our unique personalities play a key role in either limiting or expanding the number of friends we have.* Some of us prefer to maintain a larger number of less demanding relationships, while others prefer a smaller number of more committed and intense friendships.

5. *The friendships we embrace and maintain play a decisive role in determining the quality of our lives and the faithfulness of our service to God.* Friendships can be either beneficial or destructive to our spiritual and psychological well-being.

6. *It is possible for men and women to enjoy close friendships with one another without engaging in sexual contact or activities that conflict with Christian ethical and moral imperatives.* The love felt and expressed need not be romantic in nature.

7. *Friendships may cross over lines that differentiate us from others.* Most of our friends may be from our same age group, but there is no reason we cannot also develop significant friendships across generational lines. Intercultural and interracial friendships broaden our perspectives and enrich our appreciation for the global family of God.

Although we rarely experience any of these principles in isolation from the others, it is helpful to understand how each individual principle impacts specific relationships. My list is not exhaustive. What friendship principles would you add to these seven?

Step Three: Construct a Personal Definition of Friendship

The third step in developing a deepened practice of friendship involves constructing a personal definition of friendship. Your definition will be based on your unique experiences. There is no objectively right or wrong answer, but I would encourage you to try to be as specific and thoughtful as possible. Write your reflection below, attempting to limit your response to three sentences or less.

A friend is

____

____

____

____

____

____

____

Step Four: Connect Friendship to Our Spiritual Journeys

The fourth step is to relate our personal experiences to our life of faith—or, in other words, to our personal spiritual journeys. Each friendship is a spiritual journey that is launched by faith and in hope before the ultimate goal of the journey is revealed. When you meet someone, you can never know what the future holds for the relationship. The theme of each friendship journey is only revealed over time, as that journey—and that relationship—progresses.

In the Introduction, I shared my own personal definition of friendship. Let's take a closer look at it, especially in relation to what I expect from both my personal friendships and my relationships with others in my church setting:

> *A friend is a person I love who also loves me—through our linked journeys, bonds of devotion, affection, loyalty, trust, and caring grow between us, so that we desire to share our hopes, dreams, joys, and fears with each other. My friends exert influence over my heart; the deeper our friendship, the more vulnerable and self-revealing I am willing to be, and the more their opinions and feelings about me affect me. Together with my friends, I hope to fulfill God's will and change the world for Christ.*

My definition makes it clear that I'm seeking relationships that express the love of Christ. I desire friendships in which the love is mutual and freely offered. I strive to remain open to new friends whom God may bring into my life. I will welcome people of worth and character into my heart, and I pledge to bring to the relationship qualities that will make me a worthy friend. I envision relationships that will engage my friends and me on many levels: heart, soul, and mind. I hope that our sharing will be characterized by depth (and not superficiality), authenticity (as opposed to presenting a false self), and vulnerability (in contrast to posturing).

Being willing to share our authentic selves can be a challenge, even among the best of friends. We wonder: If we reveal the private aspects of our lives, will our friends still embrace us? Do we believe God will speak to our needs through them? With close friends, we must be willing to take risks, and to open our souls to another's opinions, feelings, and influence. We give our friends permission to encourage us, criticize us, and hold our secrets. Our trust in our friends makes such openness a rational, even though risky, gesture.

Friends call us to value and serve others. Our friends can also provide what each of us individually may lack—protection, gifts, wisdom, support, and graces. As the Teacher in Ecclesiastes observes:

> Two are better than one, because they have a good reward for their toil. For if they fall, one will lift up the other; but woe to one who is alone and falls and does not have another to help. Again, if two lie together, they keep warm; but how can one keep warm alone? And though one might prevail against another, two will withstand one. A threefold cord is not quickly broken. (Ecclesiastes 4:9-12)

In each of the three churches I've served as pastor, women far outnumbered men—both in terms of membership and in participation in church activities. This difference is intriguing, from a spiritual journey perspective—but perhaps it's best explained by the different ways women and men approach friendships. From a sociological perspective, Rosemary Blieszner and Rebecca G. Adams observe that women and men often provide different definitions for friendship. Women include "a loving relationship; a world of shared meanings and understandings; ongoing growth and change; the interrelated attributes of concern, sharing, commitment, freedom, respect, trust, and equality; and promotion of personal development." On the other hand, while men "also defined friendship in terms of trust and intimacy," they "emphasized instrumental activity more than women did."[2]

When applied to a church context, these findings suggest that men would tend to be more comfortable developing friendships while engaged in mission activities and projects. Mission is the aim; friendship is the benefit. Although women also emphasize the importance of mission and service to others, they tend to be more open to focusing on relationships as a core priority. Building on these insights, churches may find that the most effective way to assimilate men into congregational life is through specific service activities that also include relational and growth opportunities. Assimilating women into church life involves proactively developing relational ties, as well as offering mission and service opportunities.

Step Five: Cultivate Kingdom Friendships in Our Churches

The fifth step in deepening our practice of friendship involves connecting our personal definitions of friendship with the corporate spiritual journey of the church. How should friendships within the church epitomize the kingdom of God? Here are five premises for reflection:

1. *The kingdom of God, of which the church is a visible expression, is primarily a relational entity.* Jesus declared that the kingdom is *among* us (Luke 17:21), assuring that whenever two or three are gathered, God is in our midst (Matthew 18:21). He also declared that the world would know we are his disciples because of our love for one another (John 13:35).

2. *Those who enter the kingdom of God participate in an ongoing relationship with God, in which God is Lord and we are servants.* Friendship is not precluded by the inequality of position between God and us, because God intentionally desires mutuality with us and paves the way for it through the reconciling work of Jesus (Romans 5; Ephesians 2). This relationship is covenantal in nature, initiated solely by God's grace, energized by hope, embraced by faith, and maintained by love. It is nurtured through prayer and other spiritual disciplines and as we seek to discern and fulfill God's will.

3. *Jesus affirms that friendship is central to the kingdom of God.* He does not wish for the disciples to be merely coworkers in a movement, club, organization, or project; he clearly wants them to be *his* close friends (John 15). Furthermore, he expects them to be close friends with each other: "love each other as I have loved you" (John 15:12). In our relationships with one another, we are to discover Christ in others and express Christ's love to others.

4. *The depth and quality of the friendships Jesus' disciples establish within the kingdom of God will serve to validate the authenticity and truth of the gospel of Jesus.* Our unity is an expression of

authentic kingdom friendship and a powerful evangelistic validation of the claims of Jesus: "I have given them the glory that you gave me, that they may be one as we are one: I in them and you in me. May they be brought to complete unity to let the world know that you sent me and have loved them even as you have loved me" (John 17:22-23).

5. *Our spiritual growth requires a full range of relationships, and especially close friendships.* Vices (sin) are relationally oriented, bringing harm, alienation, and division into the world (Galatians 5:19-21). In the same way, *agape* (sacrificial love), *hesed* (covenantal faithfulness) and the fruit of the Spirit (Galatians 5:22-26) are also relational, and expressed through our friendship with God and other people. We grow as Christians by establishing and deepening relationships that express God's love and holiness. Through our friendships, we hope to challenge—and be challenged—to explore the richness and depths of Christian living.

Step Six: Build God's Church as Community

The sixth step involves imagining the kind of church community you would like to help build. I am not referring to a physical structure, but rather to the kind of friendships Jesus wants us to develop as his spiritual body.

Oscar Niemeyer was Brazil's greatest architect of the twentieth century. Although a communist and an atheist, he designed beautiful church edifices. In his autobiography, he affirmed the centrality of relationships in our lives, and he strove to embody this ideal in his architectural projects: "Here, then, is what I wanted to tell you of my architecture. I created it with courage and idealism, but also with an awareness of the fact that what is important is life, friends and attempting to make this unjust world a better place in which to live."[3]

In like manner, Paul describes the architectural design of the Christian church as a building that becomes God's temple—a site where God's people enter God's presence:

> So then you are no longer strangers and aliens, but you are citizens with the saints and also members of the household of God, built upon the foundation of the apostles and prophets, with Christ Jesus himself as the cornerstone. In him the whole structure is joined together and grows into a holy temple in the Lord; in whom you also are built together spiritually into a dwelling place for God. (Ephesians 2:19-22)

God's church finds its significance not in the physical bricks and mortar that comprise a location for meeting, but rather in the reconciling work that takes place between people in God's presence. Through Christ's death on the cross, enemies become friends and God dwells through their peaceful fellowship.

Step Seven: Ask "What Would Aristotle Do?"

Step seven involves discerning the proper motivation for joining a church, in light of the principle that the church should manifest kingdom friendships. One way to uncover the right motivation is by asking ourselves a different twist on a question that will sound familiar to most of us: *What would Aristotle do?*

Suppose Aristotle lived today and wanted to become a member of a healthy and faithful Christian church. How would he do it? It might seem strange to look to a pre-Christian (pagan) philosopher who lived more than 2,300 years ago for advice about pursuing friendship within the church. But in many ways, Aristotle is responsible for initiating Western civilization's discussion about friendship—so our thinking is informed by his insights.

Aristotle distinguished between "three kinds of friendship, equal in number to the qualities that arouse love."[4] They are:

1. *Friendship based on utility:* "Such persons do not spend much time together, because sometimes they do not like one another, and therefore feel no need of such an association unless they are mutually useful. For they take pleasure in each other's company only in so far as they have hopes of advantage from it."[5]

2. *Friendships based on pleasure:* "...their chief interest is in their own pleasure and the opportunity of the moment."[6]

3. *Friendships based on goodness (virtue):* "Only the friendship of those who are good, and similar in their goodness, is perfect.... And it is those who desire the good of their friends for the friends' sake that are most truly friends, because each loves the other for what he is, and not for any incidental quality."[7]

Which of these three different bases for friendship most reflects a kingdom view of friendship? Although many people join a church in the hopes of gaining certain benefits, I believe Aristotle would reject such utilitarian considerations. "What's in it for me?" is not a question he would want us to ask. Similarly, I think he'd caution against a community founded in friendships that exist only for pleasure. On the other hand, I believe Aristotle would join a community where the members sought for spiritual maturity and ethical virtues—not because of what they would gain from such a quest but because such a desire was their souls' desire. Indeed, who would not choose a close-knit community of virtuous people, where friendship was offered without ulterior agenda or aggressive spirit?

What would our churches look like if the people who joined them were motivated by Aristotle's third kind of friendship? In her book *Call to Commitment,* Elizabeth O'Connor shares the story of how one particular congregation—the Church of the Savior in Washington, DC—left behind Aristotle's first two categories and grounded itself in an ethos of radical love for other people. O'Connor writes:

> Before we had touched this church, most of us had chosen our friends on the basis of personal appeal, or because of

> common interests, or because of what another person did for us....When they stepped on our egos, or crossed our wills, or too often offended, we dropped them from our list....Now we are bound to a brother for time and beyond time. We resisted this kind of commitment, but the call to commitment sounded nonetheless and we knew there was only one Reconciler for that which was irreconcilable between us and a brother.[8]

When this kind of friendship animates our fellowship, transformational sharing will soon characterize church life. O'Connor recounts the formative wartime experiences of Rev. Gordon Cosby, the founding pastor of Church of the Savior. As a chaplain, he ministered to soldiers who faced death each day. What a lesson he learned after welcoming seven soldiers home, against all odds, from a dangerous night reconnaissance mission. That evening became a parable of the true church. Gordon marveled:

> "A group of people who have known that they were bound over to the power of death stumble on a treasure and that treasure is Christ. Miracle of miracles, doors that were closed open, gates of bronze are broken down. The words spill out as they try to tell one another what happened and how it happened, and of a Presence that was there."[9]

How do we cultivate this kind of intimacy in our personal relationships and in the fellowship of the church? In the next chapter, we will explore the *Friendship Circles* model, which clarifies the levels of intimate friendship we share with others.

CHAPTER 5

Exploring Our Circles of Friendship

"Some friends play at friendship but a true friend sticks closer than one's nearest kin."
—Proverbs 18:24

Professor Ray Pahl, in his book *On Friendship*, focuses on how people in today's world create and sustain their own personal networks of relationships, which he labels personal communities: "Sociologists claim that, in modern Western societies, there is a growing centrality of personal communities as opposed to geographical or work-based communities. These personal communities may be geographically scattered and may change substantially as we move through the life-course."[1] Pahl rightly surmises that this contemporary focus on friends is a significant shift away from older, conventional perspectives on communities and families.[2]

Pahl's concept of personal communities has great significance for our understandings of evangelism, church membership, and discipleship. In the past, most Protestants and Catholics selected their church based on sectarian allegiance and geographical proximity. But in a post-denominational twenty-first century, geographical proximity plays a much less important role in the choice of church membership.

From 1993 to 2003, I served as senior pastor of the First Baptist Church in Lincoln, Nebraska. The church was founded back in 1869 by city planners who believed religious institutions should play a central role in the civic life of the new state capital. So Baptists were granted a plot of land in the center of the city on which to build the church.

First Baptist Church is situated diagonally across from the state capitol building in Lincoln. For many decades this was considered to be a strategic location. However, following the advent of suburban growth and the decline of the once-vibrant downtown business district, being downtown suddenly posed significant challenges.

During my time as pastor, my home was about eight miles from the church. Regardless of what route I chose to travel to the building, I passed no less than three other churches that were closer to my home. In fact, few people in the city could claim our building was the closest church to their home. My fellow Lincolnites had to have a very compelling reason to pass other churches to get to ours.

Why would someone pass another church building to worship, fellowship, and serve Christ in our setting? They had to sense that our church offered a more compelling spiritual, relational, and mission experience than other congregations could offer them. More times than not, those people who attended and chose to stay at First Baptist either had a prior relationship with a member, or quickly developed a new friendship with a member within a few visits. Few people without such friendship connections to other members became part of our fellowship.

As we look to the future, friendship will continue to pose a significant challenge for both individuals and the church, as well as for other social institutions. Pahl writes: "Friendship is sure to grow in social and political importance as traditional forms of social glue decline or are modified. Friendships of hope could be seen as a metaphor for an enduring twenty-first-century morality."[3] People are choosing both their individual relationships and their group affiliations based on an emerging new understanding of friendship. In characterizing this new vision of friendship, Pahl notes, "At the heart of this ideal is the notion of trust. It is axiomatic that friends should not betray each other, and hence personal trust has a moral quality, although there may be limits on how far friends should support those who do transcend the moral boundaries of their particular social worlds."[4]

If trust and loyalty play central roles in the modern understanding of friendship, so does personal choice. Unlike other relationships (such as family), friendships may be freely established and dissolved. William K. Rawlins, in *The Compass of Friendship*, declares: "freedom surely lives at the heart of friendships."[5] The free-church principles of voluntary church affiliation and soul liberty are in sync with this ideal. In the interplay between freedom and trust, four key relational principles emerge:

1. *Friendships are to be entered into voluntarily, and must be mutual.* We embrace Christ because he has first loved us (1 John 1:9). In a church setting, true friendship is based on individual autonomy, choice, and trust.

2. *Discipleship relationships, such as mentor-mentee and small group assignments, must be voluntary and dissolvable by either party without recrimination.* They should also be chosen according to sound relational guidelines, and be free of all forms of coercion and manipulation.

3. *The trust we place in one another must be honored.* If breaches of trust take place, forgiveness and reconciliation should be our goal, if at all possible. Jesus modeled this for us in response to Peter's betrayal (see John 21:15-17.)

4. *The freedom to choose one's church friends does not justify discrimination or prejudice.* James prohibits discrimination on the basis of economic circumstances (James 2:2-4). The Jerusalem church enjoyed ethnic and cultural diversity and strove to promote unity (Acts 2–6).

If all this sounds vaguely familiar, perhaps that is because Jesus lived out this model of friendship two thousand years ago! In chapter two, we recreated Jesus' circle of friends and discovered that his social network was based on trust, loyalty (to God and one another), and freedom of choice. Jesus chose his friends freely, and they had the choice to journey with him or not. They were of varying ages and professions, and came from different hometowns. Some were male, but surprisingly (in light of his culture), many were female. Some friends were closer to Jesus than others. Jesus enjoyed a rich personal community that was characterized by friendships of hope.

Modern sociological inquiry, coupled with the example of Jesus' vibrant personal community of friendships of hope, encourages us to explore our own experiences. Specifically, two questions emerge:

- How do we construct our personal communities and choose friends of hope?
- How should the church respond to Jesus' call to evangelize and make disciples as a community of friends of hope?

The rest of this chapter will respond to the first question, while chapters six and seven will focus on the second question.

Visualizing the Four Circles of Friendship

There are limits to the number of people to whom any of us can offer our love, attention, support, and time. It's simply impossible to develop deep and intimate friendships with every person we meet. British anthropologist Robin Dunbar has observed that for most of human history, individuals were capable of maintaining an upper limit of about 150 friendships, defined as genuine social relationships in which we know and are known.[6] We may know the names of even a thousand more people, but we will not have an emotional attachment to all these people.[7] Subsequently, other researchers have posited that a more accurate number would be between 220 and 250. Technological advances (such as the Internet, e-mail, social networking websites, and worldwide availability of cell phones) have the potential to expand our web of relationships still further. Certainly, it is much easier to maintain long-distance friendships than it once was.

However, our ability to connect technologically to many people does not necessarily mean we have more friends. Many of the people we communicate with and link ourselves to are not really friends. We may not even know them in any personal way. This reality means that it is more important than ever to distinguish between *casual* relationships and *close* friendships.

Our Friendship Circles model provides a helpful way of appreciating the relational ties that bind us to others. Friendship circles allow us to map the network of relationships that surround us by placing people either closer or farther away from our hearts or souls (represented by the center or the bull's-eye). In our model there are four circles representing levels of relational closeness. Friendships are placed in a given circle based on our personal evaluation of the friendship's intensity.

Figure 2: The Four Friendship Circles

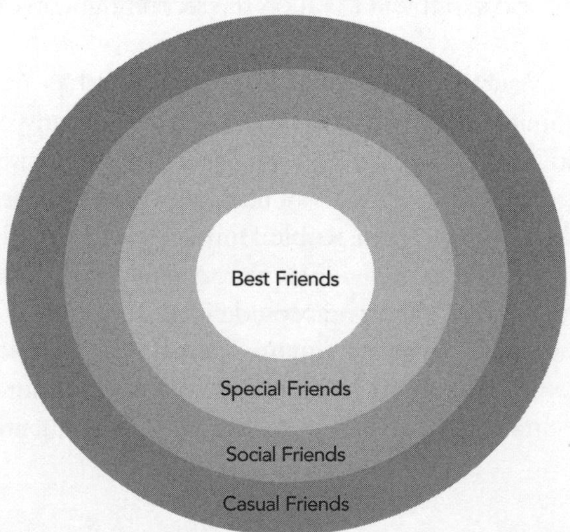

Each circle is based on the varying levels of intensity each relationship entails, with regard to trust, loyalty, self-disclosure, affection, and time:

Circle 1. Best Friends: In the center circle or the bull's-eye, we find our two or three dearest loved ones. We love and care for these people with all our hearts. These people are permitted to know many of our deepest (and most closely guarded) secrets, dreams, hopes, and fears. We want to know theirs as well. We permit them to have a decisive impact on the course of our journeys. We are willing to make extraordinary sacrifices for these people.

Circle 2. Special Friends: Here, in the second circle, we find our three to five closest friends other than those in the innermost circle. We love and care for these people with great intensity. Intimate and revealing conversations do happen with such friends. We are committed to helping and assisting these people when they have needs. We enjoy working closely with these people. We permit them to have a significant impact on the course of our journeys.

Circle 3. Social Friends: In the third circle are seven to twelve more people with whom we spend a great deal of time. We love and care for these people very much. These are the people we want to spend quality social time with, and would want to invite to smaller parties and celebrations. We permit them to have some impact on the course of our journeys.

Taken together, the members of these three inner circles constitute our *close friends*. These people, to varying degrees, have a significant claim on our hearts. The upper limit for the number of people in these three circles is approximately twenty.

Of course, each of us knows many other people with whom we relate in friendly ways and in various social settings. These people abide in the fourth circle—and beyond:

Circle 4. Casual Friends: In the outer circle are the fifty to two hundred people we know by name and with whom we might socialize or work from time to time. We like and appreciate these people, and we may or may not know a significant amount of personal information about them. Our interest in them may revolve around common interests or group affiliations. We permit them to have only a small impact on the course of our journeys.

Outside the Circles: On the periphery of our life's interactions exist our acquaintances, non-friends, and enemies.

How Do We Place People in Our Friendship Circles?

When working with people on their friendship circles, I sometimes encounter initial resistance to differentiating between levels of friendship. Because of the commitment they've made to share the love of Christ with all people, pastors and missionaries often feel especially uneasy admitting they are deeply connected to some individuals and not others. Some people feel guilty admitting they enjoy the companionship of some family members more than that of others. Nevertheless, researchers have documented that most people are able and willing to make friendship level distinctions. Pahl confirms this in his research: "Respondents have little difficulty in describing their own personal communities and in recognizing that friends can be described as having different degrees of importance and significance for them at different stages of their lives."[8]

One can find similarities to the Friendship Circles model throughout a great deal of sociological and psychological research. Various researchers frame the levels of friendship in different ways in light of their research questions. In their review of the scientific literature, Blieszner and Adams note that some researchers understand placement as a measure of "solidarity."[9] Solidarity increases as you progress toward the innermost circles and is measured by asking how important another person's opinions are to you, and to what degree you confide in them. They also cite examples of friendship distinctions such as: "acquaintance, friend, and best friend" and "casual, good, and close" friends.[10]

Intensity and solidarity are subjective feelings—though these feelings often correlate closely with objective indicators such as time spent with friends and number of secrets shared. Nonetheless, it is challenging to define each circle with precision; each person loves and cares for others in his or her own way. We can make a number of generalizations, however, that can help us place people in their proper circles:

- The greater the intensity of love, loyalty, trust, appreciation, and affection we feel for a person, the closer he or she is to the center of our friendship circles.
- The closer someone is to the center of our friendship circles, the more influence that individual exerts over our emotions, psychological health, decisions, and spiritual journeys.
- The closer someone is to the center of our friendship circles, the more pain, loss, and anguish we feel when we lose his or her fellowship or approval.
- In modern Western cultures, it's expected that a person's spouse will inhabit the innermost circle and be a best friend; however, this is a relatively new expectation, and is not always the case even today.
- Due to the intensity and demands of the relationships, circles decrease in size (can hold fewer people), the closer they are to our hearts (the center).
- Over time, friendship circles change—people come and go from them. Some may move into a more inner circle, while others may move further away from our hearts.

Do I Really Have Only Twenty Close Friends?

Twenty close friends may seem like a small number of deep relationships, but a survey of sociological research indicates that most adults do not fill up their friendship circles.[11] For example, consider these findings from Robin Dunbar's research:

> Studies which ask people to list the names of everyone whose death tomorrow they would find devastating consistently yields totals of 11 to 12. Similarly, studies that ask people to list the names of their intimates—say, those friends and relations whom they contact at least once a month—typically yield values in the order of 10 to 15.[12]

My own research confirms that adults typically fill between one-third and three-quarters of their three inner circles. Among American Baptist missionaries, more than half (54 percent) were *not* able to fill their friendship circles after arriving in their field of service. For the purposes of the study, full circles equaled 80 percent of the ideal of 20 people (sixteen or more close friends). The average missionary reports having fifteen close friends, meaning that his or her circles are three-quarters full. One-third of the missionaries, however, reported having fewer than thirteen close friends.[13]

In the friendship circle analysis for Jesus in chapter two, we listed eighteen people as close friends. Taking into account that we could have easily missed one or two close friends whom Scripture does not mention, or that Nicodemus or even Jesus' mother Mary arguably could be included in circle three, it is fair to say that Jesus enjoyed a full set of friendship circles on Palm Sunday.

My Friendship Circles model evolved from my reflections on Jesus' friendship circles. Having found the model helpful in appreciating my own experience with my friends over the course of my lifetime, I began incorporating it into my pastoral and spiritual direction ministries in the early 1980s. Since then, I have watched hundreds of people gain deeper insight into the relational dynamics of their lives.

Five Friendship Circles Principles

There are five principles flowing from my experience with the Friendship Circles model that may assist us in gaining a deeper appreciation of our personal community of friends:

■ *The Stability Principle:* The longer a person maintains a presence in one of our friendship circles, the more value that person has for us. This is due to the accumulation of experience and memories.

■ *The Empty Circle Principle:* A circle that is only partially full contributes to our sense of loneliness, but if a circle is completely empty, the impact is much greater and places stress on the other relational circles.

■ *The Full Circles Principle:* If we have close to twenty people in our three inner circles, we will experience contentment in our relationships and not be troubled significantly by feelings of loneliness.

■ *The Inner Circle Principle:* If our innermost (best friend) circle is empty, we will experience a troubling and persistent sense of loneliness, regardless of how the other circles are filled.

■ *The Best Friend Principle:* Some people prefer just one person to fill their innermost circle, while others may have two or, at most, three. When there are two or more, each must exercise a distinctive and complementary function, if the arrangement is to last and be beneficial to all.

Creating Your Personal Friendship Circles Analysis

Now I'd like to invite you to complete your own Personal Friendship Circles Analysis, using the first five exercises found in the appendix at the end of this book. (The reader may photocopy the exercises only for personal use.)

Exercise 1: Jesus' Friendship Circles—As a warm-up exercise, revisit the friendship circles of Jesus presented in chapter two. Do you disagree with me regarding the placement of any of the key people in Jesus' life? If so, re-create Jesus' friendship circles according to your own reading of the Gospels. Alternatively, select another moment from Jesus' life and fill in the circles using data from the Gospels and your own imagination.

Exercise 2: My Current Friendship Circles—Based on the description of the friendship circles in this chapter, place your friends in the appropriate circles. Try to adhere to the numerical guidelines for each circle in order to sharpen your skill in discerning between the friendship levels. Only individual names should be placed in circles one, two, and three; group designations may be used for friends in circle four (such as "my church small group" or "my work friends"). When you have completed the exercise, look for significant patterns, such as the ratio of male to female friends, the number of family members in the circles, and the number of long-term and long-distance friends. What insights do you gain from considering your circles of friends? What questions arise in your mind because of the exercise? Are you satisfied with what you see?

Exercise 3: My Current Friendship Circles—By Groupings—As you filled in your current friendship circles, you probably noticed that many of your friends cluster into groups (like work friends, church friends, etc). Shift your friends within each circle so that they are now in the most appropriate slice of the pie. There are three "slices" without categories so that you can add customized labels.

Exercise 4: My Current Friendship Circles and Social Networking Sites—Some of your current friends may relate to you on Facebook or other social networking sites; others don't. Divide your friends according to this distinction, and then do a little math to discover what percentage of each of your friendship circles is relating to you in this way. How useful are social networking sites for maintaining your close friendships?

Exercise 5: Social Networking Sites and My Online Web of Relationships—Take a closer look at your online web of relationships. How are all these people related to you? Use the steps outlined in exercise 5 of the appendix to examine these relationships further. You may discover that many of your online “friends” are actually not friends at all!

Having completed the Personal Friendship Circle Analysis, we can now focus our attention on how our friendships impact church life, evangelism, and discipleship.

CHAPTER 6

Circles of Friendship and the Journey of the Church

"Therefore, since we are surrounded by so great a cloud of witnesses, let us also lay aside every weight and the sin that clings so closely, and let us run with perseverance the race that is set before us."
—Hebrews 12:1

When I was in seminary, I performed my field education assignment as a youth minister in the first American Baptist congregation Lois and I ever attended and joined—Trinity Baptist Church in Lynnfield, Massachusetts. We entered fully into all aspects of the life of that incredible church. The "sanctuary" (which was really the fellowship hall) featured chairs arranged in a circle, to encourage us to take one another into loving and prayerful account as we worshiped God. We praised God and saw the faces of the other worshipers. Under the pastoral guidance of Rev. Howard Keeley, members of the church were regularly encouraged to join a small group for fellowship, service, and discipleship.

Lois and I were overjoyed when we were invited to join one of those groups. We were also a little anxious, because the other group members comprised much of the inner circle of the church—the key lay leaders, along with the pastor and his wife. We were the youngest couple by almost two decades! Our fears were soon overcome by the warmth and acceptance of the others. They were all delightful people—engaging, creative, intelligent, and mature in the faith. Lois and I first encountered the teachings of the Church of the Savior in Washington, DC, through a book our group studied together. I have quoted from that book for thirty years—in sermons and in this book as well!

The small group also formed the nucleus for one of the most exciting intergenerational Christian education experiments I have ever been involved in. For nearly two years, we cooperated with one another to write and teach an original curriculum designed to engage learners from kindergarten to age ninety in a joyous and theologically challenging discovery process. Each week was filled with surprising activities in which seekers of all ages were equal in the educational journey. Lois and I will never forget the series our group created based on C. S. Lewis's *The Lion, the Witch and the Wardrobe*.

Most of all, Lois and I experienced the depths and riches of committed Christian friendship among disciples eager to take risks in order to grow in Christ. No subject was off limits, and no discussion was permitted to hinder the growth of our friendships with one another. Primarily through that group, my mentor, Howard, and his wife, Hazel, became two of our closest life-long friends.

The Church "Surrounds" Our Friendships

Rebecca G. Adams and Graham Allan, in *Placing Friendship in Context*, assert that those seeking to understand the meaning, purpose, and value of friendship must not ignore its sociological dimensions. We must consider "the broader *contexts* in which such relationships are embedded" because these contexts "*surround* friendships."[1]

The church finds strength and encouragement from its past. The "cloud of witnesses" in Hebrews 12:1 refers primarily to the host of faithful people who have journeyed before us. Someday, we who are running the race presently will be included in that number. The saints of the past are part of the church's surrounding context and provide a spiritual foundation for the life of the present and future church.

The church also serves as a present-day sociological context for friendship, surrounding those relationships by serving as both network and community.[2] Our churches mold, enhance, and sometimes hinder the development and progression of our friendships. From a spiritual journey and friendship circle perspective, a church organizes and frames our journeys. Since God usually links our journeys to others, the church's life and ministries bring people in and out of our friendship circles.

The Church's Physical Surroundings and Friendship

Blieszner and Adams note that the environments in which people gather affects possibilities for friendship and the deepening of ongoing friendships. Recognizing the "competing needs for social interaction and privacy," social scientists have observed that some physical spaces facilitate interaction, while others inhibit it.[3] The spaces that nurture interaction tend to be those that bring people together and yet still allow the option of privacy—both of which are vital to developing new friendships.[4] In other words, when meeting new people, most of us like to have a place that offers room for social mixing as well as for personal space.

These observations have many implications for how we design and use our church buildings. We need to ask ourselves questions such as:

- Do our sanctuaries, fellowship halls, and Sunday school rooms help people meet one another, develop friendships, and grow those relationships?
- Do our church buildings provide spaces for both public social interaction and more private conversation?

- Do the pastor's office arrangements allow for both privacy and safeguards against inappropriate activities?
- Do our buildings afford access for people with physical limitations, so they may participate fully in the life and activities of the church?

The Church's Spiritual Surroundings and Friendship

In the New Testament, the people who gather together are the spiritual "building" that is the church (1 Corinthians 3:9-10; Ephesians 2:21; 1 Peter 2:4-10). The walls that "surround" us are spiritual and relational in nature. Faith is the necessary spiritual quality for entering into a personal relationship with God (Ephesians 2:8-10). When we place our faith in Christ, we invite his presence into our lives and commit ourselves to being open and vulnerable. Of course, this sounds a lot like friendship! When we place our faith in others in the hope that they will become our friends, we trust them.

So, *faith in Christ and trust in others* describes the attitude we must adopt to create a church fellowship that is spiritually and relationally positive. If spiritual growth is to take place, this faith and trust must be followed by companionship, discipleship, and outreach (Ephesians 4:14-16).

If the church is to make progress in attaining spiritual and relational maturity, we must take into account various tensions, which William K. Rawlins labels "dialectics."[5] These tensions describe the dynamic environment of a church as it moves through the process of forming relationships; in other words, these dialectics surround us. Consider these tensions Rawlins describes (with my own application of them within a church setting):

1. *The "dialectic of individuation and participation."* Church members are individuals with unique spiritual journeys, yet they are also involved in the larger spiritual journey of the church.

2. *The "dialectic of the private and the public."* Our relationships with others are complicated. A church friend may also be a family member, a coworker, or a colleague in another organization.

3. *The "dialectic of the ideal and the real."* Both our society and the church may promote "cultural ideals of friendships" that do not match what we experience in reality. Further, these cultural ideals may not be in line with the values of God's kingdom.

4. *The "dialectic of the freedom to be independent and the freedom to be dependent."* In denominational life (especially in the Baptist tradition) and within individual churches, the competing values of autonomy and interdependence clash. How do we maintain personal relationships when disagreements threaten the group's identity and cohesion?

5. *The dialectic of "affection and instrumentality."* All friendships, including those in the church, offer psychological, social, and spiritual benefits. Are we relating to others because they can help us, or for simply who they are?

6. *The "dialectic of judgment and acceptance."* As we grow closer to friends, we discover their quirks, idiosyncrasies, imperfections, sins, and faults—and they become privy to ours as well. As a reconciling community, the church provides an environment where we may represent ourselves as sinners saved by grace who are open to forgiveness and acceptance by others. In turn, we pledge to bear with one another's faults, to forgive, and to accept. However, we do not pledge to facilitate self-denial and self-deception, or rationalize immoral behavior and make excuses for ongoing sinful behavior.

7. *The "dialectic of expressiveness and protectiveness."* Many personal issues should be shared only with close friends, while other issues may be addressed with a wider audience. We protect not only ourselves but also our friends by exercising discretion in what and how we share. For example, sharing sensitive information about a friend's health in a prayer meeting can easily become fodder for gossip and violate that person's dignity and privacy.

Surrounding God's People with Health and Faithfulness

Rawlins's seven dialectical themes impact the church's life and mission in many ways. In our church consultation work, our regional pastoral team encourages churches to appreciate how God is working in and through the congregation's web of relationships. In essence, we probe congregational dynamics by asking two fundamental questions:

1. *How spiritually healthy is the congregation?* In our perspective, spiritual health refers to the interior dynamics of church life and relationships. It focuses on how individual members are supporting and cooperating with one another.
2. *How faithful is the congregation to its mission?* Faithfulness in mission concerns the congregation's relationship to its surrounding community and the world.

I have put together the *Endless Possibilities Health and Faithfulness Survey*, which invites church members to reflect on how well their fellowship is doing in regard to fourteen specific journey themes (seven health themes and seven faithfulness themes). The survey is an effective and user-friendly strategic planning instrument, but we will use it here as a reflection tool to discern how well friendships within the church are producing a healthy and faithful community of believers.[6]

Finding Friendship in a Healthy Church Community—A healthy congregation attracts new members by providing a safe environment for spiritual growth and positive personal relationships. Above all, a healthy church manifests God's love, as Scripture states, "For this is the message you have heard from the beginning, that we should love one another" (1 John 3:11). In the book of Acts, the Jerusalem church "surrounded" its members with a healthy spiritual environment (see Acts 2:42-47). Jesus' followers in Jerusalem ate together, shared possessions as if they were family, and spent a great deal of time with one another. What great friendships they enjoyed! Like the Jerusalem church, healthy congregations today move beyond superficial friendliness by dedicating themselves to deeper and more committed friendships.

How healthy is your church? To help you reflect on this challenging question, honestly assess how much progress your church has made in exemplifying the seven marks of a healthy church. Rate your church on a scale of one to five in each area. One equals crisis (terrible); two equals below average (poor), three equals average (acceptable), four equals above average (very good), and five equals excellent (near perfection!).

1. *Unity:* United churches manifest both loving friendships (members enjoy being with one another) and harmony and peace (members journey together with mutual respect to fulfill God's will).

2. *Worship:* Regardless of its style, authentic worship both flows from the heart (people open their hearts to God's presence and God's Word) and meets the spiritual needs of participants. Also our people expect to experience well prepared and well executed services. Authentic worship helps people grow in their affection for God.

3. *Discipleship:* Healthy churches encourage their members to engage in Bible-centered learning (especially in small groups) and to embrace spiritual practices that draw them closer to God (e.g., prayer, silence, solitude, and journaling). People are growing in their friendship with Jesus.

4. *Relationship with Pastors:* Members foster a loving relationship with their pastors by appreciating and encouraging leadership. The church promotes members' cooperation with the pastors, so that all may contribute to a trusting community of faith.

5. *Spiritual Gifts:* The church recognizes members' giftedness by helping them identify and develop their ministry gifts. It is also well

organized, with leadership that intentionally provides service opportunities for members.

6. *Caring:* Church members exhibit openness and compassion by embracing people of other races, cultures, and age levels, and by reaching out to visitors and people in need.

7. *Future-faith:* Members have hope (they are forward-looking and expect God to bless them), vision (they are implementing positive plans for future growth and service), and joy (they express a deep appreciation for God, life, one another, and the church).

What do your ratings tell you about the health of your church? Does your church excel in any given area? What areas do you think need improvement?

Congregational Health and Your Friendship Circles—Since the spiritual health of a church reflects the quality and depth of the friendships among its members and with God, the Friendship Circles model can serve as a tool for helping us discern how integrated we are into the fellowship of our own congregations. Questions you may wish to ponder include:

- How many church members are in your circles, and how deep are those friendships?
- How are your friendships affecting the overall life of the church?
- Which marks of a healthy church are you and your friends positively impacting?
- In what areas might you and your friends be negatively impacting the quality of the church's fellowship?

Practicing Health: Our Friendship Circles and Discipleship—Paul discipled Timothy. This was a natural outcome of Paul's friendship with several generations of Timothy's family. Paul encouraged Timothy to continue the chain of relationally based education in the faith: "And what you have heard from me through many witnesses entrust to faithful people who will be able to teach others as well" (2 Timothy 2:2). In our polling of pastors and lay people in congregations of our region, discipleship generally scored the lowest among the health themes. Exercise 6 in the appendix at the end of this book is designed to help you discern discipleship possibilities for you and others in your web of relationships.

Use the charts found in the appendix to explore discipleship possibilities among your current friends. Regroup the friends currently in your friendship circles according to these four categories: friends who could disciple me; my spiritual peers; friends I could disciple; and friends (whether Christian or not) who are not likely to be open to entering into a discipleship experience at the present time. Into what quadrant do the majority of your friends fall? What about your inner circle friends? What insights do you receive by seeing your friends clustered from a discipleship point of view?

If you are not presently in a discipleship relationship, consider asking one of the people in the upper left quadrant to become a mentor for you. Seek to learn from that person's experience and wisdom, and use your talks with him or her to probe questions of faith and practice so that you may grow closer to Christ. This discipleship relationship may last for as long as you and your mentor find it mutually beneficial and positive.

If you are not presently in a small group, consider asking those found in the upper right quadrant to form one with you. As a group of spiritual equals, you should negotiate the covenant of the group at the start of its journey. This covenant might include the journey theme or focus of the group, expectations for the frequency and timing of meetings (such as once a week for six months), and behavioral expectations. Members of the group should take turns hosting the meetings and leading the spiritual conversations or lessons. If the group wishes, it could ask for a more mature person to serve as a convener and facilitator.

Alternatively, you might wish to ask one or two of your peers to serve as an accountability partner. Agree to meet regularly and focus your conversations on issues of faith and the progress or roadblocks you are experiencing in your spiritual journeys.

Consider helping others grow in their relationships with Christ. Pray for each of the people in the "friends I could disciple" group, asking God to open up a window of opportunity to serve one of them as a mentor or journey encourager. You might even decide to take the initiative and invite one of them to enter into a discipleship relationship with you.

What about the people who are in the lower right quadrant—your friends who might not be willing to enter into a discipleship experience at the present time? We'll focus on them in our next section.

Enjoying Friendship through Faithful Mission

A faithful congregation embraces and fulfills God's call to bring the gospel of Jesus Christ—in all of its dimensions—to its community and to all peoples. It faithfully manifests God's kingdom through obedience to four comprehensive Scriptural mandates:

1. *The Prophetic Requirement:* "He has told you, O mortal, what is good; and what does the LORD require of you but to do justice, and to love kindness, and to walk humbly with your God?" (Micah 6:8)

2. *The Golden Rule:* "In everything do to others as you would have them do to you; for this is the law and the prophets." (Matthew 7:12)

3. *The Two Great Commandments:* "'You shall love the Lord your God with all your heart, and with all your soul, and with all your mind.' This is the greatest and first commandment. And a second is like it: 'You shall love your neighbor as yourself.' On these two commandments hang all the law and the prophets." (Matthew 22:37-40)

4. *The Great Commission:* "Go therefore and make disciples of all nations, baptizing them in the name of the Father and of the Son and of the Holy Spirit, and teaching them to obey everything that I have commanded you. And remember, I am with you always, to the end of the age." (Matthew 28:19-20)

These four mandates have one thing in common: They recognize the priority God places on being in a right relationship with our Maker as well as our neighbor. If we as individuals and as church communities practice the art of friendship with both God and other humans, all four visionary statements may be fulfilled.

With the same scale of 1 to 5 used in the earlier exercise, assess your congregation's progress in living out the following seven mission-related marks of a faithful church:

1. *Evangelism:* Members help others experience God's grace and find a spiritual home by inviting others to church.
2. *Social Action:* Your congregation expresses God's love by serving the poor, conducting ministries of social justice to improve communities, responding to emergencies (such as natural disasters and refugee needs), and caring for the environment.
3. *Global Mission:* Your church supports vocational missionaries, has a sister relationship with a church from another country, and engages in short-term cross-cultural mission trips.
4. *New Church Planting:* Your church is connected to a new church, serves as a host church to a new church, or is giving birth to a new church.
5. *Youth Ministry:* The church includes every age group in all aspects of church life (worship, music, education, outreach), and prepares its youth for leadership in the church and the world.
6. *Accessibility:* The congregation embraces and includes people with disabilities, providing all people with encouragement in their spiritual growth and opportunities for service and leadership.

7. *Giving:* Members express joy in supporting the ministries of the church and its mission partners, a sacrificial attitude in giving to God's work, and generosity as they share their time, talents, and financial resources.

Now review your rankings. How faithful is your church in living out its God-given mission? What areas are strengths for your fellowship? What areas need improvement?

Congregational Faithfulness and Your Friendship Circles—The faithfulness of a church to its mission is dependent upon the cooperative friendships we form, both inside and outside the church. Consider these questions:

- What church mission activities are you involved in, and which of your friends are working with you?
- What mission activities are you participating in that are not linked to your church? Which of your friends are working beside you in these efforts?
- Is there a mission theme that you feel led to get more involved with? Which of your friends is already connected to that theme or might be willing to join with you?

Practicing Faithful Mission: Our Friendship Circles and Evangelism—Evangelism has been practiced in many different ways. Crusade-style campaigns, literature-based evangelism, television and radio programs, Invite-a-Friend Sundays, seeker-sensitive worship services, special church events, revival meetings, and small-group studies have all been employed with varying degrees of success.

In the twenty-first century, I am convinced that every Christian has an opportunity to be a significant agent of influence and change via his or her web of relationships. Our friends naturally are disposed to pay attention to what we want to share and to take our concerns seriously. Yet many Christians are leery of sharing their faith with friends, not to mention strangers. It takes courage to risk rejection and the possible disruption or weakening of a friendship because of the stand we take for Christ. Nevertheless, being a witness for Christ entails sharing God's offer of salvation—forgiveness of sins, reconciliation with God and others, and hope of eternal life—with those friends who have not yet placed their faith in Jesus.

Exercise 7 is designed to help us explore our web of friendships in light of our evangelical mandate. (You'll find it in the appendix on page 154.) Exercise 7 asks you to evaluate where your friends are in their own journeys of faith. Are they dedicated believers in Jesus? Are they nominal or cultural Christians—people who may go to church on occasion but don't seem to make faith a central concern of their lives? Are they adherents of a different faith, or have they rejected all belief in God? Regroup your web of friendships to discover the distribution pattern of your friends with regard to Christianity. Pay special attention to your inner circle of friends. What insights do you receive by seeing your friends clustered from an evangelism point of view?

Make it a habit to pray for your friends in the cultural Christian and non-Christian sections of the circles. Each of your friends has specific hopes, dreams, and concerns that shape his or her relationship with God. Pray for your friends in light of these issues and needs, while also looking for opportunities to serve them in loving and unselfish ways. Pray that the Holy Spirit would draw them to Christ, and that the Spirit would use you in the process.

Also be prepared to share your faith when appropriate, and tailor your gospel approach to the hearer. In relationship with cultural Christians, you might emphasize God's radical commitment to us as deserving a comparable commitment. In conversation with nonbelievers or friends of a different faith, you might ask about their perspectives and invite them to do the same with you. The course of a friend's spiritual journey determines when, how, and what you might share: "But in your hearts sanctify Christ as Lord. Always be ready to make your defense to anyone who demands from you an accounting for the hope that is in you; yet do it with gentleness and reverence" (1 Peter 3:15-16). Remember that answering a question *before* it has been asked rarely produces a positive result!

Widening Our Circles

So far, we have focused our attention on those who are already present in our friendship circles. In the next chapter, we will discuss approaches that can help us expand our network of friendships. We desire our friendships to grow, both quantitatively and qualitatively. The Friendship Circles model will suggest ways to expand and enhance our discipleship and evangelistic-related friendships.

CHAPTER 7

Will You Be My Friend?

"I am a friend to all who fear you,
to all who follow your precepts."
—Psalm 119:63, NIV

The Monday afternoon Bible study at Seaview Baptist Church was a stable and faithful small group that had been meeting for years. Its members were older women; some were married while others were widowed. Occasionally, men were invited to attend as guests. It was self-sufficient in terms of leadership, and all its members were dedicated and mature Christians.

Three years into my pastorate at Seaview, I was invited to join the group for four weeks to facilitate lessons on prayer and spiritual disciplines. The four weeks turned into four years. Joining that small group transformed my relationships with these special women—most of whom were at least twice my age. As their pastor, I had had their respect. But years of meeting together gained me their affection and friendship, and I was blessed by being integrated into their fellowship circle.

Years later, I still remember them well. Each day I wake up to see a Unicorn Tapestry reproduction they bought for me when I took them on a field trip to the Cloisters Museum in northern Manhattan. The artwork is a favorite of mine; when I shared that it was close to my heart, they purchased it without my knowledge and surprised me with it at the conclusion of the day's travel. I entered into their circle of friendship, and they entered into my heart and soul.

This is the kind of friendship we all desire within our churches, but we may not always experience it. How can we form and nurture rich friendships within our church families? In this chapter we will explore three key questions that deal with the joys and challenges of inviting others to journey into and within our circles of friendship:

- How do we open up our friendship circles so that new people may explore Christian discipleship in relationship with us?
- How do we invite non-Christians into our friendship circles without compromising our faith and witness?
- How do we relate in respectful and appropriate ways to people of the other gender? Do we value them as members of our friendship circles?

Friendship and Strength of Ties

Many churches traditionally close their communion services by gathering in a circle, holding hands, and singing, "Blessed be the tie that binds our hearts in Christian love; the fellowship of kindred minds is like to that above."

Of course, not all ties are created equal. We enjoy closer ties to some people than others. Some of the friends in our circles are also good friends with others in our web of relationships, while we have other friends who may not be acquainted with anyone else in our friendship circles. Similarly, within churches, not all relationships are equal. We are closer to some church members than others; some we know quite intimately, while others may just be friendly faces on a Sunday morning.

Sociologists investigate these relational differences by referring to two concepts: *friendship density* and *the strength of ties*.[1] Friendship density refers to how tightly related the friends in an individual's web of relationships are to one another. If you have a dense friendship circle, this denotes that there are many cross relationships; people in your circles are friends with one another as well as with you. The ties between these people are said to be strong. A less dense friendship circle describes a set of relationships in which your friends are close not to one another but only to you. In this case, the ties are said to be weak.[2]

The friendship density and strength of ties within our circles impact our ability to encourage discipleship-focused relationships. Friendship density and strength of ties also shape our ability to engage in evangelical outreach, but in a different manner. There is an irony at play here—the forces that facilitate discipleship may hinder evangelism, and vice versa.

Friendship Circle Ties and Discipleship

Generally speaking, *discipleship thrives in a group that exhibits high friendship density and strong ties*. Jesus and the twelve disciples are a case in point. Discipleship is a spiritual journey that requires trust, vulnerability, and a willingness to share one's heart, mind, and soul with others. Accordingly, close friends of like faith make excellent accountability partners and discipleship group members.

This does not mean we cannot expand the number of people with whom we can grow in Christian maturity. There are multiple ways to address this issue. Let's take another look at our results from two of the previous friendship circles exercises as a way to help us discern likely candidates for just such a spiritual adventure, and then prayerfully consider the people each option reveals.

Current Friends by Grouping—First, let's take another look at the results from exercise 3 in the appendix, in which you grouped the people in your current friendship circles into several different categories. As you look again at your results from that exercise, consider how your ties to each of these groups might help you and others grow in discipleship:

1. *Church Friends:* The most obvious partners for a discipleship journey are those who already attend your church! Review this slice of your friendship circles. Starting from the innermost circle and working outward, consider each person as a possible discipleship partner. Which friends are ready and willing to join you in a discipleship journey? If there is more than one, consider forming a small group.
2. *Work Friends:* Your discipleship partners can come from outside your church. You can have a spiritual conversation partner or small group over lunch or breakfast, or even meet after work. Be careful that others in your workplace do not feel you have formed an exclusionary clique.
3. *Neighbors and Social Friends:* Consider opening your home to host a Bible study or book discussion. Keep the group as informal as possible so it doesn't feel like a meeting. Serving good food is almost always a must in this setting!
4. *Non-local Friends:* Geographic distance is not the barrier it once was. Today, it's possible to embark on a discipleship journey with friends around the world. With Skype, you can talk to friends and use its screen-sharing feature to see the same Bible text, video, or file. Serious Bible study is facilitated by websites such as www.youversion.com, which combines social networking, blogging, and Bible reading features.
5. *The Multi-slice Option:* You may be tempted to gather people from across the slices for a small-group experience. If friends from your work join in a study with church members, perhaps the work friends may decide to join your church. Although this may happen, it is just as likely that your friends from each slice of your life will favor people they already know and be less open to the others. Strong ties will work against weak ties. (You may be able to

counteract this if you include other bridge-building friends—those who, like you, are part of both groups.)

Current Friends and Discipleship Possibilities—Before we move on and talking more about evangelism, let's also consider briefly the discipleship possibilities revealed in your results from exercise 6. This exercise suggests discipleship opportunities among at least two of the groups:

1. *Spiritual Peers:* Forming a discipleship group from among your peers usually feels natural. Choose a focus that will challenge you all to grow spiritually, and have some source of spiritual wisdom—either a good book or a group facilitator (perhaps from the "friends who could disciple me" quadrant), so the group does not degenerate into merely an opinion-sharing group.

2. *Friends I Could Disciple:* Consider helping an individual friend or a group of friends grow closer to Christ under your guidance and direction. This could have benefits for you as well. Most teachers will agree that they learn a great deal when they have to prepare lessons for others.

Friendship Circle Ties and Evangelism

Many of us have visited churches where the relationships between members are so strong that they seem to have no time or inclination to reach out and make new friends when other people visit. The members of such churches will say their church is very friendly, and indeed, that is what they experience—because the friendship circles of the members are dense and the ties are strong. What they do not realize is that strangers are not easily invited to enter into the relational closeness of the members, so visitors experience the church as closed, cold, and uninviting. Visitors are given the message that they are not welcome to join, and even if they do, they may not be admitted into the friendship webs of the longtime members. In such churches, evangelism is very difficult indeed!

In contrast, "low density" churches have members whose friendship ties are weak. The people in these congregations tend to have many friendships with people who are not yet a part of the church, and may have friendships with only a few people within the church. Weak ties are characteristic both of newer churches and of churches that are growing rapidly. Churches with low density and weak ties often find it easier to evangelize and reach new people for Christ, but may have difficulty in encouraging people to join small groups devoted to discipleship and spiritual growth. The level of trust between church members may not be high enough to form groups where authentic self-revelation takes place. They are strangers to one another even though they worship together. In such churches, retention of members can become a problem; there may be an inflow of new people coming in the front door, while others silently leave through the back.

Sociologist Mark Granovetter observes that ideas spread to new groups of people through weak ties rather than strong ones.[3] At first, that may sound counterintuitive. And it's true that if I wish to influence my own group to adopt a new idea, leveraging my strong ties will quickly spread the message throughout the high-density group. However, few people outside the group may be influenced. In contrast, if I can convince a friend with weaker ties to my own circles of friendship to share my idea with her or his friends, my idea will spread rapidly to people I previously had no contact with!

Accordingly, strong ties aid discipleship but frustrate evangelism, while weak ties further evangelism but may have little immediate impact on discipleship. Jesus' discipleship group succeeds because it is a high density group with strong ties between its members. However, there are not many instances in the Gospels where that group is described as seeking to expand its size! When Jesus wants to spread the word about the kingdom of God, he achieves success by leveraging weak ties. The woman at the well quickly and effectively spreads Jesus' ideas to her own village (John 4:28-30, 39-42)—without having attended a single class on evangelism! Jesus heals a man with leprosy, then sternly orders him not to talk about it before going to the priests, and the man promptly disobeys Jesus and spreads the news all over the town (Mark 1:40-45)—a fine example of viral marketing in the first century!

A look at your results from friendship circles exercise 7 might suggest two ways you could direct your evangelistic energy. One approach focuses on the non-Christian friends already within your circles of friendship and looks for opportunities to share with them (see chapter six). The second approach looks beyond those individuals to groups they are involved with that are currently outside your web of relationships. This approach seeks to leverage your weak ties.

First, take some time now to review your friendship circles in response to exercise 7. Which people share the fewest relational ties with the others in your circles? One way to discern this is to draw lines connecting the names of people who are in relationship with one another. The people with the least connections on your chart are not necessarily unpopular; they just have weak ties with the rest of your network of friends. If you could see their friendship circles, you would discover many people to whom they could introduce you—thus giving you the opportunity to make many new friends. In contrast, the people in your web with strong ties will have many more people in their friendship circles that are the same as yours. You are already friends with many of their friends.

Second, discern the weak-tie relationships that may give you the best opportunities for evangelical outreach. Let's consider each of the three groups in the exercise: dedicated Christians, cultural Christians, and non-Christians.

Dedicated Christians with weak ties to your other friends may be able to introduce you to new groups, but many of these new people are likely to be Christians already. A physician and his family joined the First Baptist Church in Lincoln on the same Sunday my family did, and we soon became close friends. He invited me to speak several times to a Bible study group comprised of doctors. Through this invitation, I met many new people, but they were already dedicated Christians. However, if your dedicated Christian friend has not been a Christian for a long time, it's more likely that she or he may be able to introduce you to groups of non-Christians that still remain in her or his circles.

Cultural Christians with weak ties will likely have a significant number of non-believers in their circles. Even if these people are not active in a community of faith, they may be open to joining a Bible study or discussion group focused on spiritual themes. In Lincoln, our Wednesday Night All-Family Dinner and Bible Study served as a non-threatening and attractive draw for people in this category. Being somewhat familiar with the church setting, these people felt comfortable in a larger group (where they did not have to participate actively if they did not choose to) that was studying interesting topics taught in a dynamic style. An invitation from a friend was sufficient to get them through the doors of the church.

Non-Christians with weak ties to the people in your friendship circles very likely will have many other non-Christians in their circles of friendship. What a mission field! The main evangelistic challenge with this group is often the relatively wide lifestyle gap that may exist between you and the others. At First Baptist Church in East Providence, Rhode Island, my weak-tie relationship with a few teenagers led to a number of their unchurched friends coming to the weekly youth meetings.

Be sure to pursue these new relationships in the right spirit. Your motivation will soon become apparent to most, if not all, of the new people you meet. Do not use or manipulate others, and never forget you are dealing with people who have a right to be treated with respect, love, and care. You should only pursue relationships because you appreciate and value the people you encounter, and because you hope to discover new friendships. In each new friendship, you will have the privilege of listening to and learning about another person's life and journey. If you approach others with authenticity and integrity, they will be attracted to you and will desire to know what is important to you. This is when sharing Christ is a natural response on your part; if you have been a good friend, others might just listen with an open heart and mind, and welcome your witness.

Friendships with Non-Christians

To what extent should we initiate, maintain, and sustain friendships with unbelievers? Our contemporary pluralistic culture glorifies diversity, inclusivity, and integration. Friendship with those who differ from us (culturally, religiously, ethnically) is unequivocally commended. From a Christian perspective, cultural and ethnic diversity within the church is clearly affirmed at Pentecost and throughout the book of Acts.

However, both the Old and New Testaments also express ambivalence toward believers entering into friendships with nonbelievers. On the one hand, Judah enjoys a friendship with Hirah the Adullamite (Genesis 38:12,20), Naomi welcomes Ruth into her immediate family and the wider Israelite community, King Hiram of Tyre and David relate to one another on "friendly terms" (1 Kings 5:1), and Solomon and the Queen of Sheba share deeply with one another (1 Kings 10:1-13). On the other hand, Israel is forbidden to "seek a treaty of friendship" with Edom or Ammon (Deuteronomy 23:6), and centuries later Ezra wages war against intermarriage between the Jews and the neighboring Gentiles (Ezra 9–10; note especially 9:12). The various prohibitions are not expressions of ethnic, racial, or cultural prejudice, but instead are measures taken to keep Israel from embracing idolatry (Deuteronomy 13:6-11).

In the New Testament, Jesus doesn't seem to mind being accused of being "a friend of tax collectors and 'sinners'" (Matthew 11:19; Luke 7:34). Yet James worries about getting too close to those who maintain a non-Christian lifestyle: "Adulterers! Do you not know that friendship with the world is enmity with God? Therefore whoever wishes to be a friend of the world becomes an enemy of God" (James 4:4).

As a Roman citizen who traveled widely, Paul no doubt had many Jewish and Gentile friends (and some adversaries as well!). Yet Paul echoes the Old Testament concern about friendships and idolatry: "Do not be yoked together with unbelievers. For what do righteousness and wickedness have in common?...What does a believer have in common with an unbeliever? What agreement is there between the temple of God and idols? For we are the temple of the living God" (2 Corinthians 6:14-16, NIV).

So then, how can Christians be friends with non-Christians? Ezra, Paul, and James worry that deep friendships with non-Christians may cause us to fall into spiritual unfaithfulness. This is a serious issue, and the point is well taken. However, if we do not have any significant relationships with non-Christians, we cannot practice Jesus' form of friendship evangelism. Is it possible to maintain significant friendships with non-Christians without ceding influence over our spiritual convictions, priorities, and values?

The friendship circles model offers balanced guidance in this situation because it differentiates between levels of friendship based on the degrees of influence we permit friends to exercise over our souls and hearts. For friendship evangelism to be possible, at the very least we must permit non-Christians into Circle 4. Similarly, if friendship evangelism thrives on social closeness, Circle 3 friendships with non-Christian neighbors, coworkers, fellow students, and hobby or activity co-enthusiasts, need not pose a threat to the sanctity of our lives, the integrity of our witnesses, or the faithfulness of our journeys. Jesus demonstrates this by having a personal relationship with Matthew (Matthew 9:9-11). His outreach to and friendship with Matthew leads to his inclusion in the band of disciples. I would place Matthew in Jesus' Circle 3. When did he really convert—before Jesus went to his home or sometime after? We don't know, but he was in Circle 3 throughout Jesus' ministry.

Circles 1 and 2 are different. In these circles, we gift our friends with the ability to exert great influence our lives, and we should exercise extreme care in choosing whom to invite into these coveted relationships. Paul's use of the word *yoke* in 2 Corinthians 6:14 makes us think of marriage, the covenant relationship in which one soul is united with one's spouse (permitting deep influence). As commonly understood, this text establishes that Christians should only marry Christians; by analogy, deep friendships should only be extended to those who are in a position to promote our journey of faithfulness.

What about a person who converts to Christ and has preexisting non-Christian friendships in Circle 1 and 2 (perhaps including a spouse, family friends, and non-family friends)? In reference to marriage, both Paul (1 Corinthians 7:10-15) and Peter (1 Peter 3:1-7) counsel Christians to stay in the relationship in order to sanctify it. A non-Christian spouse should not be rejected, but should be loved into faith if at all possible. The spouse should not be forced out of the circle occupied before the conversion. If the spouse leaves the relationship because the person has become a Christian, the Christian may accept the decision and move on.

The principle may be extended to other friendships. New Christians should not rashly or arbitrarily dismiss non-Christian friends from their circles—unless those people are clearly evil or destructive people. Over time, as our witness grows and matures, some non-Christians will on their own volition opt out of friendship or move to an outer circle; others may even accept our testimony and become believers!

Frank Talk about Male-Female Friendships

Can men and women be close friends with each other?

Women and men throughout the centuries have been attracted to one another on many levels. Historically, marriage has been the primary way adults experience deep love and companionship with the other gender. But from childhood, children experience loving and committed relationships with people of another gender—they bond to parents, siblings, grandparents, and extended members of their families, male and female alike. They also play with and form significant relationships with children of their own age across gender lines. Accordingly, it is natural for us to wish to engage in male-female friendships as adults.

Cultures from all times and places have looked upon adult male-female friendships with caution and even imposed severe restrictions on them. The reason for this is obvious—deep relationships between men and women complicate other relationships, especially marriage. The possibility of friendship morphing into romance is always present unless clear and consistent behavioral boundaries are set and observed by both parties. Nevertheless, the dangers and pitfalls of male-female friendship have not prevented most of us from entering into such friendships.

In a personal letter written to his son Michael in March 1941, J.R.R. Tolkien expressed doubt on the possibility of male-female friendships among adults. Locating the discussion in the biblical fall of humanity, he cautions his son to lower his expectations concerning friendship with women: "This 'friendship' has often been tried: one side or the other nearly always fails. Later in life when sex cools down, it may be possible. It may happen between saints. To ordinary folk it can only rarely occur. . . ."[4]

In a post-fall world, temptation abounds and must always be taken seriously. No friendship of any kind is easily sustained or nurtured, and it can be vanquished through a moment's carelessness or sin.

How do platonic friendships compare to romantic relationships? Surely, friendship and romantic relationships share much in common. Love, appreciation, caring, and sharing characterize both forms of relationship. Spending time together, talking, engaging in activities and empathetic listening deepen both relationships. Commitment—covenant loyalty and fidelity—lie at the heart of both relationships, and they both thrive on trust. Both may be destroyed by betrayal.

There are also important differences between the two forms of relationship. According to Kathy Werking, the goal and practices of platonic friendship differ from those of romantic relationships in four ways:

1. *Platonic friendship is based on "an attraction of the spirit."* Typically, strong sexual attraction is not present—or it is strictly rejected.

2. *Marriage is not the goal of platonic friendship.* The platonic friendship "is an end unto itself rather than a means of achieving a greater goal."

3. *Platonic friendship is a relationship between equals.* The two individuals "have equivalent behavioral opportunities, and the same behavior is considered appropriate for both." Historically, men and women often had unequal roles in romantic relationships, with men having more options. Modern forms of platonic friendship, as well as equalitarian marriage models, challenge this.

4. *A platonic friendship is not an exclusive relationship.* These friends "expect their partners to engage in other friendships [or] romantic relationships. . . ."[5]

In summary, platonic friendships and romantic relationships express commitment, appreciation, and attraction in different ways, perhaps most significantly in Werking's fourth observation: romance calls for exclusivity, whereas friendship welcomes other commitments.

Given these realities, how do we initiate, develop, encourage, and facilitate morally pure and ethically positive male-female friendships within the church context? The dangers are painfully obvious; we have all heard stories about supposedly platonic relationships that have developed into illicit romantic affairs. These affairs hurt not only the two individuals involved directly, but also their families, church friends, and non-church friends. Yet the church's response cannot be to ban all relationships across gender lines. This is impossible and unrealistic. The challenge for the church is to develop wise counsel so that male-female friendships may flourish within the ethical boundaries of Christian faith and practice. Here are seven guidelines to advance the discussion:

1. *Recognize that the gender difference is a positive aspect of the friendship.* It is not possible to enjoy a close relationship with a person of the other gender without having that difference play at least an unconscious role in the relationship (such as an appreciation for the masculine/feminine characteristics that differentiate you from that person).

2. *Keep the friendship platonic (non-sexual).* It is possible for men and women to enjoy close friendships without engaging in sexual contact or activities that go against Christian ethical and moral imperatives. The love felt and expressed need not be romantic in nature.

3. *Handle sexual feelings and advances forthrightly and morally.* If both partners are single and one feels a sexual attraction, the other person has the right to either accept or reject the possible change in the relationship (from friendship to romance). If one or more of the friends is engaged or married to someone else, under no circumstances is it acceptable to act on the sexual attraction. If the person who feels the sexual attraction cannot or is unwilling to refrain from moving the relationship in a more romantic direction, the friendship should either be weakened (moved from an inner circle to an outer one) or ended.

4. *Know the difference between sharing secrets and being secretive.* Inner-circle friends naturally become more self-revealing as the relationship progresses. The secrets we reveal concern our hopes, dreams, fears, and insecurities. When such vulnerability is accepted and honored, deep trust and love develops between friends. This is what makes friendship so rewarding! However, friends must not give in to the temptation to become secretive about their relationship. Friends who are in an honorable relationship do not need to meet in secret. Nor should they ever imagine that their relationship is so special or unique that it is allowed to break Christian norms of holy conduct.

5. *When one or both friends are married, the spouse's feelings, opinions, and comfort level must be respected.* Platonic friendships should not negatively affect marriage relationships. Both friends have a responsibility to "monitor" the friendship so that each knows its impact on his or her spouse and family.[6] Friends should make every effort to include their spouses in the friendship, even if the relationship with the spouse is not as deep. At the very least, the spouse should be willing to express support of the friendship, and should be kept abreast of its developments and course. In a healthy marriage (one that is not characterized by jealousy, manipulation, or psychological abuse), the spouse has a right to express any concern he or she may have about the friendship, and those feelings should be respected and addressed.

6. *Friends need to be aware of how their friendship is perceived and interpreted by others.* Werking says friends must be engaged in "successfully handling the public's perceptions of the friendship."[7] This is especially true in a close-knit community like a church! If friends receive feedback indicating that it appears as if they are dating, acting romantic, or cheating on their marriages, then they must adjust their actions to rectify the perceptions—whether they believe

these perceptions to be accurate or not. In such situations, we should be attentive and responsive to any feedback we receive from other close friends, since they can offer valuable insights and perspectives about our blind spots or when we are in denial.

7. *Friendships not only deepen and mature, but also weaken and die.* This is true for all platonic friendships, whether they cross gender lines or not. Unlike marriage, where the Bible indicates the commitment should normatively be monogamous and lifelong, the duration of a friendship is uncertain—and unknown to us—when it begins. It is never easy to say goodbye to a relationship that has been significant to us, but we must accept that our friends retain the right and privilege of weakening or pulling out of a friendship with us. Platonic friendships should be weakened or ended when they negatively impact a marriage, when one of the friends becomes uncomfortable with the sexual dynamics of the relationship, or when key journeys held in common conclude or diverge.

Werking observes that friendships require "structural opportunities" in order to develop and succeed.[8] Church life offers many places where men and women can interact with one another in ways that are conducive to platonic friendship. Many, although not all, small groups in churches include both women and men. Other groupings, such as choirs, music teams, and age-level or special-interest ministries are also open to people of both genders. Such contexts provide a safe haven for non-romantic friendships between men and women.

CHAPTER 8

Journeying Together: A Spirituality of Friendship

"If then there is any encouragement in Christ, any consolation from love, any sharing in the Spirit, any compassion and sympathy, make my joy complete: be of the same mind, having the same love, being in full accord and of one mind."
—Philippians 2:1-2

New Englanders are not known to be an expressive people, especially in public. They can be reserved and reluctant to talk about certain subjects, such as religion, money, and politics. So I was surprised when I encountered a great deal of affection from the members of my church in East Providence, Rhode Island. I was not prepared for the kindness many showed me after our Sunday worship services; I'd never received so many handshakes, hugs, kisses, and smiles as I did when worshipers exited the sanctuary each Sunday morning. Nevertheless, I always interpreted their affectionate displays as an appropriate way to relate to their pastor in public.

Friendship and Holy Kisses

Paul encourages the church to greet one another with "a holy kiss" (Romans 16:16; 1 Corinthians 16:20; 2 Corinthians 13:12; 1 Thessalonians 5:26). Holy kisses express greeting and welcoming. Clearly, Paul was not asking church members to engage in romantic activity in public; he views appropriate physical contact as a symbol of Christian friendship and fellowship.

Holy kisses underscore the gospel's insistence that Christianity is an incarnational religion. In Jesus, God becomes close to humanity. Jesus touches us, and can be touched by our plight. Jesus experiences maternal and paternal love, friendships with both men and women, and, with Judas in particular, the pain of a close friend's betrayal. How sad and ironic that Judas betrays Jesus with a kiss, taking the symbol of spiritual friendship and perverting it!

Judas's kiss in the Garden of Gethsemane paves the way for Jesus' trial and death. Subsequently, among the people who follow Jesus, a simple kiss paves the way for life in the Holy Spirit, in which love, unity, and holiness are expressed in and through the friendships of Christian pilgrims. The holy kiss invites the seeker to enter, through baptism, into the journeys and friendship circles of both God and the church.

Throughout church history, Christians have recognized the profound spiritual significance of friendship. In a wonderful set of arguments that echoed the familiar biblical maxim that "God is love," the twelfth-century Christian monk Aelred of Rievaulx boldly proclaimed: "God is friendship!" Although the context for Aelred's thinking was medieval England and the monastic community, he offers valuable insights for twenty-first-century Christians who believe the church should be a community of friendship and that such friendship finds its origin in God.

Aelred's concept of friendship is completely Christ-centered: "For what more sublime than can be said of friendship, what more true, what more profitable, than that it ought to, and is proved to, begin in Christ, continue in Christ, and be perfected in Christ?"[1] This threefold progression—friendship that *begins* in Christ, *continues* in Christ, and is *perfected* in Christ—is more than just a set of good talking points for a contemporary three-point sermon! It represents the classical spiritual journey paradigm, a model of the Christian life in which a Christian grows into Christ in three successive stages: *purgation* (the forsaking of worldly life and sin at the beginning of the Christian life, as symbolized by baptism), *illumination* (the progressive elevation of the soul as it ascends towards heavenly existence through steps of sanctification), and *union with God in Christ* (the heavenly spiritual union of the soul in perfect love, harmony, and purity).[2] Any monk of Aelred's day would have been familiar with such thinking. Further, they would have understood that friendship with God is essential for one's spiritual journey. Aelred writes:

> And so in friendship are joined honor and charm, truth and joy, sweetness and good-will, affection and action. And all these take their beginning from Christ, advance through Christ, and are perfected in Christ. Therefore, not too steep or unnatural does the ascent appear from Christ, as the inspiration of the love by which we love our friend, to Christ giving himself to us as our Friend for us to love, so that charm may follow on charm, sweetness upon sweetness and affection upon affection. And thus, friend cleaving to friend in the spirit of Christ, is made with Christ but one heart and one soul, and so mounting aloft through degrees of love to friendship with Christ, he is made one spirit with him in one kiss.[3]

What personal characteristics should a friend have in order to be admitted into the inner circles of our hearts? Aelred has a ready answer: "There are four qualities which must be tested in a friend: loyalty, right intention, discretion, and patience, that you may entrust yourself to him securely."[4]

Journeying with God, Our Friend

How do we journey through life with God, our friend, and with one another? Friends share with one another and engage in common activities. Human friendship thus mirrors the heavenly and eternal fellowship of the Trinity and advances God's will on earth. The eternal Godhead creates the universe; our friendships change the world for the better. Friends project the goodness of their personal relationships into their respective webs of relationship and even beyond into society at large.

When God is our friend, we are invited to participate in a set of spiritual journeys. In 1997 I wrote a book describing the *Endless Possibilities* paradigm for understanding our spiritual journeys.[5] I believe spiritual journeys emerge from God's interaction with human beings through time. Each spiritual journey is an expression of God's friendship with us, and our cooperation with God advances us along that journey. Let me say a bit more about spiritual journeys in general, before tying it back to the specific theme of friendship.

According to the *Endless Possibilities* paradigm, each journey is defined by a *theme*, and each theme represents God's will for a portion of our life. Journey themes might include things like serving in a church or organization ("God has called me to teach senior high Sunday school this year"); work or professional activities (ministers are not the only ones whose work qualifies as a divine vocation); relationships with others (each relationship exemplifies a theme that defines the importance of the relationship—such as being a husband or a father); or personal growth (psychological, spiritual, and intellectual).

God leads us through a *five-phase* progression in order to fulfill our journey themes:

1. *Preparation:* God prepares us to embrace and live out an aspect of his will by giving us the life experiences, relationships, knowledge, and wisdom necessary to set out on the journey. Moses' forty years in the desert prepared him for the burning bush; Paul's experiences as a Pharisee prepared him to become an apostle.

2. *Call:* God reveals a journey theme, often expressed as a goal.

Moses at the burning bush, Jesus' baptism, and Paul's Damascus Road experience are but three examples.

3. *Cooperation with God and Others:* God links our journeys to others so we may help them reach their journey goals, and they can help us reach ours. We cooperate with Jesus by acknowledging him as the Lord of our journeys. Cooperation is a hallmark of friendship.

4. *Reaching the Goal:* A journey comes to an end when you fulfill its goal! Jesus' death on the cross is an example of this phase. Resigning or retiring from work and completing a mission assignment or board term for a church are common examples.

5. *New Life:* We are not the same people at the end of a journey as when we began it. Participating in a journey changes us; completing one journey prepares us for the next one God has in store for us. After Jesus dies, he rises to new life; the interim period between the cross and his ascension represents phase 5 of Christ's journey.

All our spiritual journeys progress according to these five phases. Knowing a journey's theme and the phase we are in helps us determine if we are making progress in fulfilling God's will—and if our friendships with God and others are bearing fruit.

A comprehensive spiritual journey paradigm, such as *Endless Possibilities*, balances inner spiritual growth with other-centered service. Journeys that focus on our personal and spiritual growth goals are called *redemptive* journeys (see Romans 12:1-2). Journeys that focus on changing the world for Christ are called *mission* journeys. The *Health and Faithfulness* survey tool that we considered in chapter six applies these journey perspectives to congregational life. The health themes are lived out through a church's redemptive-level journeys, while faithfulness themes are exemplified by the church's mission-level journeys.

With that framework in mind, we turn our attention back to friendship, and ask this question: What kind of a journey is friendship? Is it redemptive- or mission-level? Is friendship more about our own spiritual growth (redemptive) or is it about bringing about God's kingdom in our world (mission)? I would suggest that with regard to our friendship with God, our journeys have a redemptive aim. Befriending God changes us, so that we progressively become more Christ-like. Paul says, "For to me, living is Christ and dying is gain" (Philippians 1:21). In practical terms, this means living a life that expresses the holiness of God, as modeled by Jesus: "For this is the will of God, your sanctification" (1 Thessalonians 4:3). Over time, we naturally tend to become like our friends, and adopt their virtues and values. This is certainly true in the case of our friendship with God.

When it comes to our friendships with other people, the answer is more ambiguous. There exists in human friendship a give and take that includes characteristics of both redemptive- and mission-level journeys. We help our friends, and they tend to our needs. After thirty years of reflection on this question, I have come to view friendship as the "boundary" between the redemptive- and mission-level domains of life. True friends cross the border often and in a mutually beneficial way, so that both are blessed by the give and take.

Notice that I have refrained from labeling friendship as a distinct third journey level. Although human friendships can be described nicely by the *Endless Possibilities*' five-phase outline, there is one fascinating anomaly when it comes to friendship—and it's related to phase two. In both redemptive- and mission-level journeys, we gain a fairly clear sense of the journey's goal when we receive God's call in phase two. For example, God may call us to serve as pastor of a specific church, attend a specific college to pursue a certain major, or chair a church board for a specified period of time. But when we meet other people and sense an interior call or desire to pursue a friendship with them, we usually do not know God's intention for the friendship. Will the friendship stay superficial or grow into a deep or life-long commitment? Will it remain a platonic friendship or morph into a romance or marriage? There is a mystery at work in our relationships, and only time will tell what will happen to our friendships!

Friendship and the Fruit and Gifts of the Holy Spirit

The Holy Spirit plays a significant role in our spiritual journeys. The Spirit guides us into deeper holiness, truth, and wisdom as we pursue our redemptive-level journeys (John 14:26; 16:5-15). First Corinthians reminds us that "the Spirit searches everything, even the depths of God" so that we might gain "the mind of Christ" (1 Corinthians 2:10,16). Similarly, the Spirit anoints and empowers us as we seek to fulfill our mission journeys. When Peter was "filled with the Holy Spirit" (Acts 4:8), he was able to preach with amazing effectiveness. In regard to our friendships, the Holy Spirit promotes unity within the body of Christ (Ephesians 4:3).

Paul employs two powerful images to explain the presence of the Holy Spirit in our relationships and journeys—the fruit and the gifts of the Spirit. He introduces the fruit of the Spirit after detailing personal failing and immoral lifestyle choices that Christians must forsake (see Galatians 5:18-25). Taken as a whole, the fruit of the Spirit—love, joy, peace, patience, kindness, generosity, faithfulness, gentleness, and self-control—describe attitudes and behaviors we should exhibit in and through all our relationships, in order to reflect the virtues and values of the kingdom of God. They are what Christian friendship is all about. When we seek to grow in these qualities, we are actually embracing redemptive-level spiritual journeys, where each fruit represents a journey theme or goal. When members of a church express these qualities in their relationships with each other, the church as a whole becomes healthier.

The gifts of the Spirit are enumerated in various places, and none of the lists appears to be comprehensive (Romans 12:3-8; 1 Corinthians 12-14; 1 Peter 4:10-11). I do not believe that the lists are exhaustive; the Holy Spirit is free to gift the church with whatever may be appropriate to express God's power and to accomplish

God's purpose. All the gifts should be appreciated as a means to an end: "Like good stewards of the manifold grace of God, serve one another with whatever gift each of you has received" (1 Peter 4:10). The gifts are the means by which the Spirit anoints and empowers God's people so we might serve the church and reach out to the world. In regard to our friendships, the gifts of the Spirit provide us with the tools we need to further other peoples' journeys. Exercising gifts is one of the ways we cooperate with God and others during phase three of our journeys.

The fruit and the gifts of the Spirit enable us to share our journeys with one another and thus facilitate authentic friendship. They symbolize God's desire to see our friendships blossom and the fellowship of the church reach its potential. God shares through the Holy Spirit so that we may share with one another!

Sharing Our Journeys with Our Friends

William K. Rawlins observes, "Friendships emerge among the personal, relational and cultural narratives of our lives."[6] In other words, when we share our spiritual journeys with our friends, we reveal what is significant to us, we discover what is important to them, and our friendships grow and deepen. As our friendships deepen, we also seek to include our friends in our journeys. Rawlins states:

> When we choose our friends, we not only are selecting co-actors in the stories of our lives, we are selecting co-authors and co-tellers. Poignantly over the course of our shared lives, we also come to serve as trusted curators of the stories of our friends' lives, even as they preserve our co-told and witnessed narratives.[7]

This is precisely what happened between Jesus and his disciples. As they journeyed together for three years, they spoke and listened to one another, they studied and worked together, they lodged together and ate meals as one community of faith. Toward the end, Jesus summarized the messianic theme of their journey in the Lord's Supper, and charged them to "do this in remembrance of me" (Luke 22:19; 1 Corinthians 11:24). In effect, he made the disciples "trusted curators" of his journey. The disciples accepted this call, which transformed them into "witnesses" of Jesus' messianic journey (Acts 1:8; 2:32; 3:15; 10:39-41; 13:31).

The small group of Jesus' disciples has served as a model for Christian fellowship for the past two millennia. Small groups are one of the primary ways the church strengthens the journeys of its members. These journeys are communicated within the context of friendship ("I want to tell you my story and hear yours!"), as an expression of friendship ("Let's recount and celebrate what we've experienced together!"), and as a consequence or fruit of friendship ("God is guiding me through what you have shared!"). As Elizabeth O'Connor writes: "In small groups we can create the climate and nurture the trust in which a deep giving of ourselves can happen.…What is involved is the recovery of love, itself, the communion that is the deepest need of every life, the unlocking of the infinite capacity that each one has to be a friend and to have a friend.…Unfortunately, this journey which is the foundation of the community in Christ is not well mapped for us, but it is abundantly clear that it is more easily made within a group of twelve or fewer."[8]

Small-group participation is an integral part of healthy and faithful church life, since it provides a context for our redemptive and mission journeys. When a small group's journey is redemptive, the group focuses on the spiritual growth of its own members. When its journey is mission-level, the group seeks to serve others. O'Connor suggests that small groups be made up of fewer than twelve members; yet it's clear that small groups impact not only the members of the group but also the journey of the wider church fellowship. Strong group fellowship enhances a church's spiritual health, while mission-level journeys by small groups increase the church's faithfulness.

Technology, Friendship, and the Size of Small Groups

Prior to the communications revolution, participating in a small group usually involved face-to-face encounters. Traditional small groups depended upon geographical proximity and the commitment of members to be in the same place at the same time. Today, there are alternative forms of small groups that merit serious consideration for their potential impact on spiritual formation and service. It is now feasible to hold audio or video conference calls online, which eliminates the necessity of geographical proximity. Emerging technologies, such as Google Wave, collect communication streams between groups of people over time. New members can be added at any time, and they can play back a group's online conversation to catch up.

It is not clear yet if these new ways of journeying as a group will shatter O'Connor's "twelve or fewer" small-group size restriction, but the potential is there. In groups where the sharing is less personal, group size may be enlarged through technological means. Geographical proximity seems less significant in this situation. However, just as in traditional settings, a few people may end up dominating online group discussions as group size increases.

If the group's focus is on sharing one's hopes, dreams, and fears in a vulnerable and honest way, then technological innovation may have only a limited effect. Most people will risk such sharing only with the people who dwell in their three close friend circles—ten to twenty people at most. Thus, a group size of twelve still seems like an upper limit, not only because there is a limited number of people in our circles, but also because of the time and energy required to listen to everyone else in the group.

Can we remain close friends with people who are geographically distant? At first glance, technological advances seem to solve the major dilemma of long-distance relationships—the lack of ongoing communication between friends. Through e-mail, cell phones, and Internet telephone services, we can keep up with people no matter where they live. This appears to be a wonderful solution to our problem—until we realize those same technologies also are allowing hundreds of other people to keep in touch with us as well! Out of my three hundred Facebook "friends," more than half are not really personal friends (they are not in my four circles). I have to be diligent in order to make sure the cacophony of so many voices does not drown out my true friends.

Furthermore, we need to be careful to distinguish between friends we hang on to because technology makes it relatively easy and friends who are really still journeying with us. Our affection for significant former friends, coupled with our memory of past good times, may persuade us that we remain close because the technology keeps us in superficial contact. We may need to ask ourselves if the technology is actually fostering a continued deepening of the relationship or if it's just keeping the relationship artificially alive. That said, I do believe that technology can bridge the gap between face-to-face visits of close friends who are geographically separated, but this is not an adequate long-term substitute for such close encounters.

"Holy Friendship"

Technology may or may not transform the way we maintain friendships, but the objective of Christian fellowship and friendship remains the same: "Instead, as he who called you is holy, be holy yourselves in all your conduct" (1 Peter 1:15). The call to holiness within the community of Christian friendship can be expressed in a variety of ways. We can relate to others through serving them; we can relate to others through receiving from them; we can relate to others by learning from them; we can relate to others by teaching them. Above all, we can relate to others by being authentic and sincere friends who yearn to manifest the presence and purpose of Jesus Christ. Through all of these modes of relationship, we seek to become change agents. L. Gregory Jones and Kevin R. Armstrong dream:

> Who could have the courage to see the world charged with the grandeur of God, to see the world shining like transfiguration? It would be people who have cultivated the wisdom and skill to have eyes to see and ears to hear the beauty of God, the beauty of this world, and the beauty of a congregation's life together. Such wisdom and skill are learned and lived in the friendships and practices of Christian life—because the beauty we are called to see and hear is not culturally defined but rather shaped by the Triune God's abundant, gracious, loving engagement with us and the world.[9]

God's holiness, shining through Christian friendship, can change the world. Jones and Armstrong state that, "Christians are joined to others in ways that develop over time into holy friendships. Such friendships are crucially important in helping us discern the truth of our own lives."[10] Holy friendships carry us into a deeper friendship with God and grant us the courage to confront our imperfections. Holy friendships are "oriented toward discernment and deepening of Christian vocation, as well as nurturing growth in Christian life, toward our learning how to live as holy people."[11]

Pastors, Spiritual Leaders, and Friendship

Jones and Armstrong point out that friendship is a crucial issue for pastoral leaders as they seek vocational excellence:

> When we began asking groups of pastors and laity what was most important in sustaining their work, friendship was almost always at the top of the list. A clear sense of purpose, supportive family, able judicatory leadership, and

> adequate financial resources for a life well lived are all important. But the need for good friends seems to transcend the challenges and frustrations that plague so many.[12]

Pastors are people too! It should come as no surprise that clergy have the same relational needs and aspirations as other people. Their personal spiritual health and their faithfulness to their calling depend on the encouragement, strength, and support they receive from their friends. However, being in leadership presents special challenges. As we observed in chapter one, loneliness is a significant problem for pastoral leaders.

When pastors, mentors, chaplains, missionaries, musicians, and youth workers experience loneliness—when their friendship circles are too empty—their ability to sustain faithfulness and excellence in ministry may diminish. Instead of joyfully serving others in a spirit of love, they may act out of an increasing sense of frustration and need. Relational isolation can cause tunnel vision (an impaired ability to see the totality of a situation) and lead to poor judgment and inappropriate actions. Ministerial loneliness also may tempt leaders to cross behavioral and moral boundaries, harming themselves and many other people.

Both ministerial leaders and the church members they serve bear a responsibility for combating clergy loneliness. Here are some practical suggestions for each side.

For Clergy and Other Spiritual Leaders—

1. *Recognize your own need for quality friendships.* The friendship circles exercises in this book can help you appreciate the friends you already have and spot empty or under-filled circles.

2. *Pray for discernment as you seek new friendships and manage your current friendship circles.* The friends you admit into your friendship circles will influence your personal spiritual journeys and the quality of your vocational service. Choose them wisely.

3. *Cultivate friends both from within and beyond the church you serve.* Jesus was a close friend with his disciples; in the same way, clergy may develop friendships with selected church members. Jesus also had friends who were not part of his discipleship group, and pastors should have friendships outside the church. This is especially vital during times of congregational struggle, or when the pastor's position in the church might be tenuous.

4. *Always observe professional ethical and moral boundaries.* Clergy may never use their authority and power to manipulate or violate other people.

5. *Serve your flock while appreciating the difference between loving others and being their personal friend.* Jesus loved and served all who came to him, but only a select few were permitted to enter his circles of friendship.

For Lay People—

1. *Appreciate the humanity of your spiritual leaders.* You may have been attracted to them because of their spiritual gifts, maturity, and service, but do not forget that they are just like you and thus have relational, psychological, and emotional needs and desires. Treat your pastoral leaders with respect, love, and sensitivity.

2. *Honor the need of your leaders to choose their own friends.* All people have the right to choose whom they will invite into their friendship circles. The choice of friends need not impair the ability of your pastor to serve the rest of the congregation. If you are not chosen, don't let your disappointment negatively impact your support for the pastor.

3. *Encourage your leaders to attend to their friendship circles.* Churches demand a great deal of attention and time from their pastoral leaders! It is easy for pastors to neglect their own relational needs as they seek to serve their people. Respect your pastor's Sabbath day and personal time off. Otherwise, she or he will have no time for family and friends.

4. *Attend to your own friendship circles.* Use the friendship circles exercises to maintain and expand your web of relationships, both within and outside the church. Do your best to make sure your friendships promote the spiritual health of your church and support its mission to your community and beyond.

5. *Pay close attention to your friendship with God.* The depth and quality of your relationship with God will impact all your other friendships.

Friendship Is Hard Work!

Many people perceive friendship to be a spontaneous, serendipitous, and surprising experience that just happens to us. Nothing could be further from the truth! Deep and lasting friendships require sensitive and thoughtful reflection, creative planning, and intentional actions to thrive. Throughout this book, we have been engaged in the hard work of appreciating our friendships. Now, let's take the next step—exploring friendship as a spiritual discipline.

CHAPTER 9

Friendship as a Spiritual Discipline

"Intimate union with God leads to the most creative involvement in the contemporary world."
—Henri Nouwen, *The Genesee Diary*[1]

Friendship is a spiritual discipline because it is something we can choose to practice rather than just letting it happen. Attention, conversation, and activity move friendships forward, and all three take intentional and determined practice to perfect. Our friendship with God is sustained by the other disciplines of the contemplative life (silence, solitude, prayer, Bible study, and communal worship), and is freely given away and offered to others through our evangelistic and social mission journeys.

"The Long Loneliness"

In her autobiography, *The Long Loneliness*, social activist Dorothy Day, one of the founders of the Catholic Worker movement, explains that her passion for the poor was preceded first by a deep friendship and then by a period of loneliness. Day recalls her discovery of friendship, when she meets Rayna Simons at college: "Then in the midst of the bare hardship of my days, a new love came into my life, a new love of friendship that was also as clear as a bell, crystal clear, with no stain of self-seeking, a give-and-take friendship that meant companionship and sharing."[2]

After her university years, Day followed her family to the lower east side of New York City, leaving her friendship with Rayna behind. There she encounters a profound loneliness:

> In all that great city of seven millions, I found no friends....Silence in the midst of the city noises oppressed me. My own silence, the feeling that I had no one to talk to overwhelmed me so that my very throat was constricted; my heart was heavy with unuttered thoughts; I wanted to weep my loneliness away.[3]

One might imagine that her cure would involve fleeing the city, but in a rather mystical intuition (prefiguring her later conversion to Catholicism), she senses a call to serve because of her experiences of friendship and loneliness. So begins her pre-Christian work on behalf of the poor. By the end of her journey, she grasps the spiritual implications of her service:

> We cannot love God unless we love each other, and to love we must know each other. We know Him in the breaking of bread, and we know each other in the breaking of bread, and we are not alone anymore. Heaven is a banquet and life is a banquet, too, even with a crust, where there is companionship. We have all known the long loneliness and we have learned that the only solution is love and that love comes with community.[4]

In her life-long embrace of companionship, loneliness, and social advocacy, Dorothy Day discovered the connections between love, friendship, and mission. As a Catholic, Day understood that our friendship with God and our friendship with others cannot be separated if we wish to experience authentic friendship in all of its dimensions. When we practice friendship as a spiritual discipline, our personal lives and our public witness are made one.

Friendship, Spirituality, and Service

Friendship with God and other people are the two foci of Christian spirituality. Both are relational goals that can best be realized when we immerse ourselves in our faith through the practice of spiritual disciplines. Thomas Merton offers a beautiful description of the connection between Christian spirituality, service, and friendship with God and others:

> Real Christian living is stunted and frustrated if it remains content with the bare externals of worship, with "saying prayers" and "going to church," with fulfilling one's external duties and merely being respectable. The real purpose of prayer…is the deepening of personal realization in love, the awareness of God (even if sometimes this awareness may amount to a negative factor, a seeming "absence")….
>
> What is the relation of this to action? Simply this. He who attempts to act and do things for others or for the world without deepening his own self-understanding, freedom, integrity and capacity to love, will not have anything to give others. He will communicate to them nothing but the contagion of his own obsessions, his aggressiveness, his ego-centered ambitions, his delusions about ends and means, his doctrinaire prejudices and ideas.[5]

Merton rightly asserts that our witness to the world—our social action in the name of Christ—must be grounded in authentic spirituality: "We must learn to distinguish between the pseudo spirituality of activism and the true vitality and energy of Christian action guided by the Spirit."[6] To put it another way, our friendship with the rest of humanity must grow out of our friendship with God.

The traditional disciplines of the Christian life assist us in drawing closer to God, and so prepare us for service in the world. Henri Nouwen writes, "The desert fathers did not think of solitude as being alone, but as being alone with God. They did not think of silence as not speaking, but as listening to God."[7] Having heard from God, we may then share a life-giving spiritual message to the world (John 6:43-51). Nouwen speaks of Anthony, the earliest of the desert monks, as an example of how friendship with God, cultivated through the spiritual disciplines of silence and solitude, gives birth to "compassionate" ministry. Nouwen writes:

> Here indeed is ministry in its purest form, a compassionate ministry born of solitude. Anthony and his followers, who escaped from the compulsions of the world, did not do so out of disdain for people but in order to be able to save them...Thus in and through solitude we do not move away from people. On the contrary, we move closer to them through compassionate ministry.[8]

Compassion flows from love—or, as Scripture declares, "We love because [God] first loved us" (1 John 4:19). The people who are seeking God's presence, compassion, love, and friendship come right to the doorstep of our churches every day. How will we welcome them?

Friendship and the Inviting Church

From my thirty years of experience as a local church and regional pastor, I have come to the conclusion that most first-time visitors to a church decide within ten minutes of entering the sanctuary whether they will return for a second visit. In this initial exploratory visit, newcomers assess whether they will fit in, make friends, and find a safe place to explore their faith. What fascinates me about the selection process is that it is largely intuitive, and that it often concludes before the choir has had the chance to sing, before the pastor has had the opportunity to impress with a sermon, and even before the offering plate has been passed!

If visitors feel uncomfortable after their initial 10-minute assessment, they often spend the rest of the service focusing on how and when they can escape from the sanctuary! They will locate the exits and examine the worship bulletin to discern if there is an appropriate time for them to leave early. If they are sufficiently nervous or uncomfortable, they will seek to avoid personal contact and conversation (even during the greeting time), and will monitor their own rising level of discomfort (just notice how often they glance at their watches!).

On the other hand, if visitors feel comfortable within those first ten minutes, they may focus on seeking points of contact with others in the sanctuary (hoping to find possible new friendships), look forward with anticipation to the upcoming sermon, and even peruse the worship bulletin to see where they might fit within the church's life (small groups and ministry opportunities).

A church that is sensitive to the feelings, needs, and thoughts of visitors has a greater probability of success in inviting them back for a second experience. It also will stand a greater chance of inviting visitors to explore possible new friendships.

As we seek to create church environments that are truly "friendly" to visitors, we can benefit from the work of Rosemary Bliesner and Rebecca G. Adams, who speak of three kinds of "friendship processes" through which people assess whether someone else may be a candidate for friendship:

■ *Cognitive* processes reflect the internal thoughts that each partner has about herself or himself, the friend, and the friendship. These thoughts concern such things as how one evaluates her or his performance and the partner's performance of the friend role, assesses the stability of the friendship, explains events that occur in the friendship…and so on…

■ *Affective* processes encompass emotional reactions to friends and friendship. Empathy, trust, loyalty, satisfaction, and commitment to continuing the friendship are all positive or pleasurable emotions. Indifference, anger, hostility, and jealousy are examples of negative or unpleasant emotions...

- *Behavioral* processes are the action components of friendship. They include communication...displays of affection, social support or resource exchange, cooperation, accommodation to a friend's desires, joint activities, betrayal, manipulation, conflict, competition, and the like.[9]

It's easy to see how these friendship processes influence our experience as visitors and (later) members of a church. On a cognitive level, we ask, "What do I think about this church and the people in it? Do I agree with their theology and beliefs?" On an affective level, we may ask, "How do I feel about the people I'm encountering in this church? Do I like them? Do they like me? Am I comfortable with who they are? Are there enough people who look or sound like me?" On a behavioral level, we ask: "What can we do together? Will we be able to work together on common projects and interests? Is this a place where I can grow personally and serve God faithfully?"

As we consider the challenge of making disciples from a relational perspective, we must recognize the large impact these three friendship processes will have on whether visitors will decide to make our church their spiritual home. We must ask ourselves: If the people who visit our church do decide to stay, what kind of spiritual home will they find?

Going to Church Alone

One advantage to being a pastor or guest preacher is that you're usually invited to sit at the front of the church facing the congregation. What a vantage point for observation and reflection! I don't have the statistics to prove it scientifically, but over the past thirty years I have noticed a shift in the people filling our church pews (or folding chairs) in the United States. Compared to my earliest days as a pastor, I now see fewer complete nuclear families (wife, husband, and one or more children of varying ages)—and even fewer multi-generational or extended families. Many congregations are missing entire generations of people. Churches are filled with individuals (and couples) who usually have no familial relationship with anyone else in the congregation. These folks come to church alone (even if they have family at home), they sit by themselves in the sanctuary, and they leave to eat Sunday dinner without outside company. It is very possible that other members of their households may attend another church—perhaps the parents attend a Baptist church while the oldest child attends a community church down the road.

Robert D. Putnam has documented this societal change in his book, *Bowling Alone*. Writing in 2000, he reviews the shifting sense of community over the course of the twentieth century: "Without at first noticing, we have been pulled apart from one another and from our communities over the last third of the century."[10]

Clearly, churches have not been immune from the effects of this relational riptide. Putnam reports that church membership among Americans today is down by 10 percent, and church attendance and involvement in fellowship or Christian education activities have decreased by 25 to 50 percent.[11] The friendship fabric of our churches has been ripped apart, and it is vital that we rebuild it in the twenty-first century.

Rebuilding the Church's Friendship Infrastructure

We cannot predict what the church's social life will look like one hundred years from now. Perhaps the downward trend Putnam and others have documented will reverse itself. But we cannot afford to assume a passive stance. There are many options for meeting the challenge, and there's no "one size fits all" solution to our current situation. As a general guide, I would like to share a seven-point agenda for rebuilding the church's friendship infrastructure.

First, *make a biblical understanding of friendship in particular, and relationships in general, a top priority as we disciple our members.* Both adults and children should be encouraged to reflect upon their friendship circles and apply biblical standards of love, charity, and compassion to their relationships. As part of this training, we must recapture a picture of the church as a community of Christian friends who are called to love God and others with all our being.

Second, *reaffirm the role of discipleship groups in the life of a truly healthy and faithful church.* Many churches have developed and experimented with small-group ministry, but all too often these groups lack theological focus and purpose, as well as solid leadership and direction. Pastors should devote a significant part of their ministries to leading small groups and training strong lay leaders for such groups. We need to create an expectation that every member of a church will participate in at least one small group. Each group should have its own covenant, a clearly articulated journey theme (whether redemptive or mission), and adequate educational resources (see chapter eight and *Endless Possibilities*). In general, I have found that a church should establish two groups devoted to redemptive journey themes for every mission group it sponsors. A church can give away only what it has received from God; the two to one ratio keeps a community and its individuals from burning out.

Third, *rediscover the role of hospitality in the Christian life and in making new friends.* Paul is uncharacteristically succinct when he commands: "Share with God's people who are in need. Practice hospitality" (Romans 12:13; see also 16:32; 1 Timothy 5:10; Hebrews 13:2; 1 Peter 4:9; and 3 John 8). Hospitality and friendship go hand in hand. I recall a special family at Trinity Baptist Church in Lynnfield, Massachusetts. Every Sunday, they would invite several people to join them for lunch at their home after the worship service. They were gracious hosts, and as poor graduate students, Lois and I often secured invitations! It is one thing to be invited to a church service or event; it is quite another to be asked to enter a person's home. This is essential if we hope to move our churches from superficial friendliness to authentic communities of friends.

Fourth, *embrace a lifestyle of generosity*. Paul exhorts Timothy to teach his church to excel in generosity: "Command them to do good, to be rich in good deeds, and to be generous and willing to share" (1 Timothy 6:18). Generosity in all its manifestations enhances friendship. The generosity of God sends Jesus into human history, and Jesus models generosity in his sacrifice on the cross. The Jerusalem church in Acts exhibits a generous spirit, and no doubt their generosity helped to authenticate their spiritual message.

Fifth, *develop creative meal-based ministries for both small- and large-group experiences*. Children's and adult Sunday schools are struggling in many churches, while the traditional Sunday evening service and midweek prayer meeting have largely disappeared. What can bring us back together? I like to tell the joke that in my Baptist tradition, there are three ordinances of the church—not just two. In addition to baptism and the Lord's Supper (communion), there is the covered-dish or potluck dinner! Behind my levity, there is a serious point. Sharing meals together is a hallmark of friendship. Following his resurrection, Jesus re-established fellowship with his disciples by eating with them (Luke 24:30-43). At First Baptist Church in Lincoln, we christened our midweek all-family dinner "Food for the Journey." After the meal, we offered a full range of educational opportunities. We averaged 80 to 120 participants (from small children to older adults), and many felt it was the highlight of their week. This could also be done on Sunday mornings; a Sunday school program with few children could be refashioned into a weekly all church pre-service breakfast or brunch, where intergenerational Bible study could be offered.

Sixth, *readjust sanctuary seating to maximize the worship service's friendship potential*. I often find myself preaching in sanctuaries that can seat hundreds more people than are presently attending the church. Inevitably, the attendees spread out through the sanctuary. When it's time to sing, no one can hear anyone else. Worse still, when visitors enter, this seating pattern almost guarantees they will be isolated from everyone else. The friendship potential of the service is thoroughly minimized, and the evangelistic mission of the church fatally compromised. Under such circumstances, the return of a visitor is virtually a miracle! Smaller congregations need to be trained to sing as a group, and sitting close to one another is an absolute precondition for a church service that seeks to be a credible witness to friendship. This may involve removing or rearranging seating in order to create a more viable climate for friendship. If at all possible, create a sanctuary seating arrangement so that on an average Sunday, at least 65 to 70 percent of the available seats will be taken. Increase the seating capacity when the church reaches an occupied seat level of between 75 and 80 percent.

Seventh and final, *program for ministries, not meetings*. Social isolation cannot be overcome by a committee assignment, but friends working together to alleviate a societal need can find fulfillment and satisfaction. When we join forces to contribute to a good cause, we cultivate virtue—a quality Aristotle calls us to search for in worthy friends. Dorothy Day and others like her found true community in service, especially to the poor.

Church need not be a lonely place. It has the potential to be a sacred space where the long loneliness of a lifetime can be redeemed and transformed into authentic Christian friendship and community.

CHAPTER 10

When Journeys End: Saying Goodbye to Our Friends

"But fate ordains that dearest friends must part!"
—Edward Young, *Love of Fame, the Universal Passion*[1]

Despite all his *panache*, Edmond Rostand's Cyrano de Bergerac really only desires one triumph—gaining the friendship and love of the beautiful Roxane. Thwarted by his unattractive looks, Cyrano cannot compete against the handsome but tongue-tied Christian. Christian attracts Roxane's gaze, but he requires Cyrano's poetic elegance to retain her heart. After Christian dies in battle, Roxane retires to monastic life. Though for years she enjoys his visits, Roxane never grasps that Cyrano is the true author of Christian's love letters and poetry—until their final conversation, as Cyrano succumbs to mortal wounds with these words: "In you at least I had a friend: for once I heard a silken rustle in my life." Roxane responds in despair, "I only ever loved one man, and now I am losing him again!"[2]

So, at the very end, Cyrano gains not only the friendship of Roxane but also her love. Roxane's devotion releases Cyrano, so that he can face death with all of his...*panache*!

Saying Goodbye Well

My pastoral mentor and lifelong friend, Howard Keeley, has shared a great deal of wisdom with me, especially in regard to relationships. One of his proverbs in particular has lodged itself deep within my soul, and I've repeated it in talks all around the globe: "Always say your goodbyes well!"

Unlike marriage partners, friends do not begin their common journey by declaring, "Till death do us part." Some friendships last a lifetime, but many other friendships last for just a short while, or flourish for years and then slowly dissolve. How do we say our goodbyes well in those circumstances?

Friendships end for a variety of reasons. Beverley Fehr notes that psychological research has focused on causes such as:

- Loss of geographical proximity because one or both friends move.
- One or both friends discover qualities in the other that they do not like.
- Competing demands for a friend's time or attention leave too little time to keep the friendship going.
- New friendships or romantic relationships are formed which weaken the friendship.
- One of the friends begins to feel romantically inclined, to the dismay of the other.[3]

The friendship between Judas and Jesus was ended by Judas's betrayal. Matthew records that Jesus calls Judas his friend at the moment of his arrest: "Friend, do what you came for" (Matthew 26:50). When Jesus calls Judas "friend," he is not in denial—and he certainly is not saying that Judas remains his close friend despite the betrayal. In fact, Jesus is communicating just the opposite! In John 15, when John records that Jesus calls the disciples "friends," he employs the plural form of the Greek word *philos* (as in Philadelphia—the city of brotherly love). Matthew does not use this word, but rather a form of *hetairos*. He uses this same word in Matthew 20:13 and 22:12, where the relationship being described is hardly inner circle. A better translation would be "companion." Matthew wants us to know that in Jesus' mind, Judas's betrayal has seriously weakened their friendship. They are no longer close friends. This is the last encounter between the two. Their journeys are no longer in sync, and their friendship is no longer viable.

In Acts, a serious disagreement leads to a disruption of the friendship between Paul and Barnabas. Paul plans for a missionary journey following the Jerusalem Council. However, he and Barnabas disagree over whether to include John Mark:

> Barnabas wanted to take with them John called Mark. But Paul decided not to take with them one who had deserted them in Pamphylia and had not accompanied them in the work. The disagreement became so sharp that they parted company; Barnabas took Mark with him and sailed away to Cyprus. But Paul chose Silas and set out, the believers commending him to the grace of the Lord. (Acts 15:37-40)

We could argue over who is in the right in this disagreement. Those siding with Barnabas might appreciate his family loyalty to a kinsman (Colossians 4:10) and honor his compassion and willingness to give young Mark a second chance. Others, siding with Paul, might point out that under the kind of intense spiritual warfare inherent in Paul's ministry, faithfulness and courage are paramount. Mark lacks these qualities, and having him on the team could be dangerous. They might posit familial nepotism as the motivator behind Barnabas's decision in Mark's favor.

Both sides make valid points, and certainly, Paul and Barnabas each had a right to make up his own mind about Mark's qualifications. What really matters is the impact the disagreement has on their relationship and their apostolic journeys. As far as we can ascertain, the disagreement has a negative impact on the friendship between Barnabas and Paul. They go their separate ways, and there is no record of them working with one another again. The divergence in their mission journeys signals at least a weakening of their friendship, and quite possibly its demise. How sad! Yet this is a very common experience. The faithfulness of a mission journey depends in large part upon trusting relationships among the participants. If friends cease trusting the judgment of the other partner, journeying together becomes difficult, if not impossible.

There is some good news at the end of this story. Years later, Paul apparently reconciles with Mark and resumes a working relationship with him (2 Timothy 4:11; Philemon 24).

Sin and the Disruption of Church Friendships

Jesus anticipates that it will be a struggle to maintain relationships within the church, and he supplies a process for addressing the conflict (Matthew 18:15-17). He advises that we may even find it necessary to sever ties if others won't be reconciled: "If the member refuses to listen to them, tell it to the church; and if the offender refuses to listen even to the church, let such a one be to you as a Gentile and a tax collector" (v. 17).

In an age where there was only one Christian church per community, ending fellowship with a recalcitrant church member was a severe punishment and a powerful deterrent. However, in the twenty-first century, where every community has many churches, it has lost its punch. If people are asked to repent or leave, they will most likely see themselves as victims, leave indignantly (and try to take other members with them!), and join a church down the street or in a nearby town! In the process, friendships are weakened or destroyed, and the whole church ends up suffering.

In a healthy and faithful church family, spiritual friends hold one another accountable under the Lord: "My brothers and sisters, if anyone among you wanders from the truth and is brought back by another, you should know that whoever brings back a sinner from wandering will save the sinner's soul from death and will cover a multitude of sins" (James 5:19-20). Paul echoes the same theme in 2 Corinthians, instructing that a person who repents and changes his or her behavior should be restored into the full fellowship of the church: "This punishment by the majority is enough for such a person; so now instead you should forgive and console him, so that he may not be overwhelmed by excessive sorrow. So I urge you to reaffirm your love for him" (2 Corinthians 2:6-8).

Questions to Ask When a Friendship Dissolves

We need to learn how to respond appropriately when friendships dissolve. In her book *Among Friends*, Letty Cottin Pogrebin offers a very helpful set of questions for those facing the ending of a friendship:

If you are the one ending the friendship, ask yourself:

- Have I been fair? Have I given my friend the benefit of the doubt? (Never dissolve a friendship on hearsay evidence.)
- Am I fed up with what the friend *did* or what the friend *is*? (Isolating a particular infraction and putting the rest of the person in perspective sometimes permits reconsideration.)
- If there is no chance of reconciliation, have I been firm and clear about it so that there can be no misunderstanding?
- Even though the parting is my choice, am I prepared to feel pangs of guilt and regret later?

If you are the accused and you want to fight for the friendship, think about these questions:

- Am I able to acknowledge my mistakes or explain my actions without defensiveness or rancor?
- Should I do it by phone, in writing, or in person? On my turf or my friend's? In a public place (where we are less likely to make a scene), in a restaurant (where it is harder for my friend to escape), or in a private setting?

- Do I really want to make up, or do I want to get back together so I can take revenge?
- If I resolve to change, can I keep my promise? Do I really want the friendship if I have to change? Is a clean slate possible or will we be too self-conscious?
- Can my friend and I learn to disagree on some things and still get along, or is it just a matter of time until we have another major blowup?
- How many rejections will convince me to let the friendship go?[4]

In cases where reconciliation and restoration of a friendship are impossible, Pogrebin offers one more piece of advice: "If a friend's rejection is final, do not flagellate yourself. Assume you did all you could and make a clean break. Forgive the friend for not forgiving you. Retaliation is wasted energy. You even the score best by denying an ex-friend the power to haunt you."[5]

Our Spiritual Journeys and Friendship Changes

In the *Endless Possibilities* paradigm of spiritual journeys (presented in chapter eight), the loss and gain of friends is seen as a natural part of the journey process. Each of the five phases of a spiritual journey impacts our friendships and, in turn, is impacted by our friendships.

In the *preparation phase* of our journeys, God introduces people into our friendship circles who are necessary for the faithful execution of the emerging journey. They may have the wisdom or gifts needed to make up for our own shortcomings. Other people may move out of our friendship circles, because God does not intend for them to journey with us. These friendship changes may confuse us, because we do not yet know the journey theme. When we gain or lose friends in this phase, we usually do not understand God's purpose behind the changes.

The *call phase* of our spiritual journeys involves a period of discernment in which we hear a possible call to journey (expressed as a journey goal or theme), evaluate its authenticity and claim on our lives, and either accept or reject it. Friends may play an invaluable role in this phase. They may be the mediators of the call—the ones who introduce the goal or theme to us. They may play a counseling role to help us process the potential call to journey. They may confirm the call after we have embraced it. Some friends may feel led to accept the call and journey with us, while others may decline and move in other directions.

Throughout the *cooperation phase* of our journeys, we partner with others in order to fulfill the journey themes that represent God's will for our lives. Some friendships are intended to bless only a part of the journey, while other friends will be alongside us for the duration. In part, this helps to explain why some people both join and leave church. Whether we are aware of it or not, our participation in a particular congregation's journey may be intended for only a limited time; once our part in the journey is fulfilled, we feel an inner urge to move on. To be sure, unfaithfulness to God and the journey may also cause people to drop friendships during this phase.

The *reaching the goal* phase of our journeys is the goodbye stage. We not only say goodbye to the journey itself (having reached its goal), but at the same time we also say goodbye to the friends who journeyed with us. In our own lives, graduations, retirements, and ending ministry assignments are all examples of this poignant phase.

At the conclusion of my pastorate at First Baptist Church in East Providence, I wanted to say my goodbyes well. Right after placing my letter of resignation in the mail, I hurried over to the home of one of my favorite seniors in the church. Gertrude welcomed me into her home, and silently listened to my news. I thought being the first to know would touch her heart. But all she said was: "Goodbye! By tomorrow, you'll be just a memory!" In a sense, she was right! At the end of a journey, we consolidate our memories of the journey and its participants, we celebrate its triumphs, joys, and highlights, and we learn from our mistakes. This is the phase where we express our deep appreciation for those we love and have befriended.

Having said our goodbyes well, we move on to the *new life* phase of our journeys. Strengthened by the wisdom we have gained from the newly completed journey, we begin to look forward to God's new possibilities. Who will move on with us from our past journeys? What new friends will join us? Time will tell!

Friends Move In and Out of Friendship Circles

As we move through life, we will both gain new friends and lose prior friendships. Paul lost Barnabas and John Mark, but added Timothy to his team soon after (Acts 16:1-3). Many scholars believe it was around this same time that Luke also joined Paul's circle (note the "we" in Acts 16:11).

We can use the friendship circle exercises to keep track of the movement of friends in and out of our friendship circles over time. Whenever we do the friendship circles exercise, we are taking a snapshot of our friendships at a particular moment in time. Accordingly, we can review snapshots from our past to gain an appreciation of the flow of people in and out of our friendship circles.

Exercise 8 in the appendix (see page 155) can be used for this purpose. Think back to a time right before your last major life change (relocating from one place to another, starting a new job, getting married or divorced). What individuals were part of your web of friendships at that time? Fill in the friendship circles, showing how close individuals were to you at that time. Of course, you can go further back in time, and repeat the reflection exercise for other key transition times in your life. The more snapshots you take, the more movement you'll witness. Then begin asking questions, such as:

■ Who consistently appears in my inner circles throughout my life?
■ Who moved out of my inner circles or disappeared altogether? How do I feel about losing these friendships? Why did these friendships end or weaken? Did I say my goodbyes well? Are there any people I should consider asking back into a closer friendship circle?
■ Who moved from an outer circle to an inner one? How do I feel about them? Did I welcome them properly? Are these wise or foolish friendship choices on my part?
■ Over the course of my life, am I pleased with the choices I have made in regards to my best friend and special friend circles (circles 1 and 2)? Have I chosen wisely? Have I nurtured and supported these friendships, or have I taken them for granted and neglected them?
■ As I look to the future, what friendship circle changes should I consider? Do I need to say goodbye to some friendships and hope for the introduction of new friends into my circles?

Leaving a Church and Saying Goodbye to Friends There

Most people will leave at least one church over the course of their lifetimes. In many church covenants, members are counseled to join a new church when they move away from the church they had been attending. If church membership involves being in relationship to others so we can serve Christ together, then it only makes sense to say goodbye to one church and join another if we make a geographical change.

But a change in location is not the only reason people might say goodbye to one church and the friendships they've enjoyed there and build a new relationship with another church. There are many reasons why members choose to move on to another fellowship, including spiritual malaise or boredom, power struggles, personality conflicts, discomfort due to cultural or ethnic differences, weak programming, changing ministry needs or desires, a romantic relationship where the significant other belongs to a different congregation, or theological concerns.

From a spiritual journey perspective, there may be occasions when God calls us to change congregational settings in order to pursue new redemptive- and mission-level journeys. Perhaps the life lessons or wisdom we need requires a different pastor, mentor, or church environment. A church we love may even commission us to go and start a new church plant in another neighborhood or city.

We should never leave a church to avoid confronting those issues that God, through the church, is calling us to face. We affect our circles of friendship whenever we leave a church, and we should carefully weigh the ramifications of our decision before sending shockwaves throughout our circles. A look at your results from exercise 3 (see page 149) will quickly show you the people most affected by your decision—your *church friends* slice of the pie. When considering leaving a church, ask yourself the following questions:

- Is my reason for leaving the church wise and based on my spiritual journey, or am I running away from an issue I really need to deal with?
- Who will be most affected by my move? Is the move worth losing or weakening certain friendships? Will the move isolate me relationally, or do I have enough strong relationships to help me through the contemplated transition?
- What honest feedback have I received from my close friends on my move? Have they raised any red flags or warnings?
- How can I say goodbye well so that my friends are encouraged, and how can I help my friends say goodbye to me?

Saying Goodbye Well When Friends Die

Of all the goodbyes we must say, the hardest for most people to handle is when someone we love and care for is dying—or when we are dying. Some people will do everything in their power to avoid such emotionally wrenching situations. Saying our goodbyes well in the face of death may be very challenging and difficult, but, as in the case of Cyrano and Roxane, it has the potential to be extremely beautiful, sublime, and deeply meaningful to all parties.

After journeying with his friends for about three years, Jesus choreographs his farewell to them with deep sensitivity. Jesus expertly prepares them for his death. He coaxes them out of their denial, highlights the significant journey themes they embraced together, celebrates their closeness to him, reaffirms his love for them, eats one last meal with them, prays with (and for) them, and reassures them that even after his passing, God will not leave them alone. He shares wisdom with them, reiterating old lessons and introducing new insights, and models servanthood and humility by washing their feet (John 13–17).

Jesus also expresses faith that though death may temporarily separate him from the disciples, the separation will not last. Because God is friendship and friendship is eternal, Jesus assures them that their relationship with him will survive even death: "In my Father's house there are many dwelling places. If it were not so, would I have told you that I go to prepare a place for you?" (John 14:2).

Knowing his death was near, Jesus said his farewells in a beautiful way. Facing death is a universal human experience; we all have either said goodbye to someone who has left us, or will do so in the future. How do we say our goodbyes well when faced with the death of a friend?

Based on Jesus' approach to saying goodbye to his friends, I recommend a three-step strategy for saying goodbye to friends when death threatens to conclude our relationship. This strategy relies on our practicing the spiritual art of *appreciation*. Appreciation is not synonymous with "liking" something; we do not like the fact that death is separating us from a friend. Instead, it is an active way of approaching life and all the losses it brings. It is an art we can develop through intentional practice and spiritual direction.

1. Embrace the end of a friendship—don't deny it—Contrast Jesus' words at the Last Supper with the disciples' continuing denial of his warnings about his coming death. Because the loss of a friendship can be devastating and destructive to our sense of well-being, we often remain in denial until the ending can no longer be avoided. Denial is unhelpful and ineffective as a true coping strategy; it can never deal with the reality it runs away from. Furthermore, denial magnifies the intensity of the loss when it actually hits.

In contrast, embracing loss is a very effective first step in neutralizing its harmful effects. When we embrace a loss, we turn toward it, open our arms to enclose it, and bring it closer to our heart for contemplation, consideration, and reply. We accept what it brings us and make it ours. Once the loss becomes assimilated into our consciousness, we are able to go deeper still—we are now prepared to gain some perspective by "seeing the loss."

2. See what you're looking at—Contrast Jesus' focus on his spiritual journey at Gethsemane with his disciples' surrender to sleep. When we merely look at something, we spend little energy in the activity, and we do so in a superficial way. ("What are you up to?" "Oh, I'm just looking at this magazine.") We can *look* at a body in a casket and not *see* the person who inhabited that body. We can look at a painting or photo and never see the creator's intent or point. Most of us are afraid to do more than look at the loss of a friendship; we quickly avert our gaze because of its accompanying pain. It hurts to keep looking.

In contrast, the discipline of seeing requires focus, time (lots of it, in proportion to the magnitude of the loss), and courage. When we truly see something, its significance emerges and we can engage it on that level. We begin to perceive connections, themes, and the emotions or feelings our soul associates with them. Affirming the importance of a loss is vital to learning the lessons our friendships embody. Seeing completes its work when we gain wisdom and insight into the meaning of a friendship.

3. Search for hidden beauty and depth—Don't flee out of fear— It is one thing to accept a loss (embracing) and to learn from it (seeing), but it is quite another to appreciate it deeply! However, that is exactly what God calls us to, as Jesus himself demonstrates through the cross. Calvary is the epitome of loss, and on many levels, a horrible tragedy (an innocent person is painfully executed). This is why the disciples flee and desert Jesus; the loss crushes their hopes and dreams. Who can blame them?

Since the resurrection and ascension of Jesus, we now see Jesus' death in a totally different light (the one that Jesus perceives before his death and which draws him to that end). Paul calls us to contemplate the sufferings and death of Jesus so that we will go beyond the physical pain and discover (in a mystical or experiential way) the hidden beauty and depth of Jesus' sacrifice (Philippians 3:10-11). It is more than important or significant; it is beautiful and it is the greatest piece of art ever created by God. Similarly, when we are able to discover the hidden beauty at the core of the loss of a friend, that loss is stripped of its negativity and repulsive energy. It becomes a work of art that attracts us because we sense that a loving God is at work in the midst of our pain. When this hidden beauty is found, appreciation becomes its own reward, and our friendship is transformed into a treasured memory.

A Time for Friendship

The author of Ecclesiastes wrote, "For everything there is a season, and a time for every matter under heaven: a time to be born, and a time to die; a time to plant, and a time to pluck up what is planted" (3:1-2). Between birth and death, we human beings are blessed with the gift of friendship from God. Throughout our years, friendships are birthed, and we glory in their blessings. What brings more bliss than the companionship of good friends who love us? When our friends die, we rightfully mourn and are comforted. The memory of a good friend is balm for our souls.

Like the heavens, good friendships declare the glory of God. Like God's law, godly friendships revive our souls, give joy to our hearts, and provide light to our eyes. The best friendships are more precious than gold and sweeter than honey. And whenever we share in a true friendship in this life—and in the world to come, there is great reward (Psalm 19:1-11).

CONCLUSION

The Future of Friendship

"Instead I hope to see you soon, and we will talk together face to face. Peace to you. The friends send you their greetings. Greet the friends there, each by name."
—3 John 14-15

One of the draws of Facebook and other social networking sites is the possibility of reconnecting with old friends. Sometimes lost friendships can be rekindled, but often the reconnection fizzles after just a few short interactions. Once rehearsing the past has been exhausted, there's nothing left to say. Friendships cannot survive solely on past memories, but they do thrive on the hope of future sharing, growth, play, and activity. Without a forward-looking hope, a friendship has no future.

Hope plays a decisive role in our friendship with God. Paul declares, "we rejoice in the hope of the glory of God" (Romans 5:2, NIV). We have hope for the future because we believe our friendship with God will deepen, grow, and reach its fulfillment in Christ:

> Blessed be the God and Father of our Lord Jesus Christ! By his great mercy he has given us a new birth into a living hope through the resurrection of Jesus Christ from the dead, and into an inheritance that is imperishable, undefiled, and unfading, kept in heaven for you, who are being

> protected by the power of God through faith for a salvation ready to be revealed in the last time. (1 Peter 1:3-5)

Daniel Schwartz has explored the focus on hope and friendship in the writing of Thomas Aquinas. Schwartz notes that Aquinas believed hope is a "theological virtue" that is "causally prior to charity/friendship."[1] In other words, hope is a precondition for friendship. Schwartz writes:

> Faith, hope, and charity, the three theological virtues, are conceived of by Aquinas as stages in a process reaching its fulfillment in friendship with God.... God is first loved as a benefactor, and only at a later stage is loved irrespective of the benefits He confers. If a human being disbelieves in his capacity to be worthy of these benefits, and so despairs, he will be unable to conceive of God as his own personal benefactor. He will fail to experience the interested love which ultimately, according to Aquinas, becomes friendship. It is hope therefore that makes friendship possible.[2]

Hope not only makes friendship possible with God; it also affects our human relationships. When we link our journeys with others, we express hope. For Aquinas, friendship relies upon two forms of hope: "the hope that the common goal will be accomplished" and "the hope that the friend's feelings, affections, and intentions, which sustain the relationship, may continue in the future."[3] Schwartz concludes, "These two hopes sustain each other just as the hoped-for things do: friendship makes possible the achievement of the goal, and the existence of the goal makes the friendship possible."[4] The success of our spiritual journeys depends upon the quality of friendships we develop with others. Furthermore, our journeys provide the context for our friendships to grow and be blessed.

Hope launches our friendships and our journeys into the future. We will embark upon a journey only if we are hopeful that its goal can be fulfilled. When we establish a new friendship with someone, hope is essential in giving us the faith and courage to invite that person into our lives. As a relationship develops, hope convinces us that sharing in a vulnerable way is a reasonable risk to take. If we are going to chance suffering rejection, we want to hope that we might actually succeed in gaining acceptance.

As the body of Christ, we need to examine the structures of church life to ascertain whether or not we have created environments in which hope promotes the development and deepening of our friendships with God and other people. Is hope expressed when we gather as the people of God? Do our worship services bring us closer together or reinforce our isolation? Do our small groups provide a safe environment for the sharing of joys, concerns, achievements, and failures, or do they encourage us to play a religious game in which we give the correct answers and remain at a superficial distance from others? When visitors come to our churches, do we greet them lovingly and with hope—or with reserve and fear?

Churches can advance the cause of Christ by training people in the fundamental skills of friendship—how to share authentically and appropriately, and how to listen attentively and sympathetically. There are times when it is appropriate to share what is happening in one's life in a self-revealing and vulnerable manner. At other times, we might be tempted to disclose something in an inappropriate manner or to share secrets best kept private. The extent of our sharing should be correlated to a friend's place in our friendship circles. In like manner, as we listen to others, it may be appropriate to offer advice or counsel; at other times, the most appropriate response may be sympathetic silence or quiet support. Sensitivity can be taught and modeled. Henri Nouwen states:

> To be a teacher means indeed to lay down your life for your friends, to become a "martyr" in the original sense of witness. To be a teacher means to offer your own faith experience, your loneliness and intimacy, your doubts and hopes, your failures and successes to your students as a context in which they can struggle with their own quest for meaning.[5]

Imagine what it would be like if each and every one of our churches became a place where sharing on multiple levels was encouraged and people knew how to listen appropriately and respond hopefully! Such a gathering of disciple-friends surely would be attractive to seekers of authentic Christian community.

A Future for Friendship

Throughout this book, my aim has been to listen to and share a conversation spanning millennia. Since the time of Aristotle and the biblical writers, the subject of friendship has engaged philosophers, theologians, monks, nuns, prophets, scientists, songwriters, novelists, poets, playwrights, psychologists, and sociologists.

Now our generation has the opportunity to contribute insights and perspectives to the conversation. We may also redefine the practice of friendship. The twenty-first century is a stage on which personal autonomy and relational interdependence will dance together. Advances in technology and communications have the potential to extend and expand our circles of friendship. No longer do "communities" of people need to be geographically defined, for in a virtual world shared interests can bind people more closely together than physical proximity.

These changes and trends will challenge and inspire Christian churches as we experiment with innovative ways to practice discipleship and evangelism in our day. I hope the *Endless Possibilities* spiritual journey paradigm, the *Friendship Circles* model, and the *Health and Faithfulness* congregational life and mission assessment tool will help our churches address friendship-related issues in a creative manner.

Despite all the changes humanity is experiencing in the beginning decades of the twenty-first century, one thing remains perfectly clear: Friendship still is, and will always continue to be, a central feature of human existence. Our hearts yearn for friends. Our minds dream about the possibilities, promises, and pitfalls of friendship. Our souls are willing to take extraordinary risks to experience true and authentic friendship. Cicero, who next to Aristotle, has had the greatest influence on the course of the long conversation on friendship, exclaims: "All I, myself, can do is urge you to place friendship above every other human concern that can be imagined! Nothing else in the whole world is so completely in harmony with nature, and nothing so utterly right, in prosperity and adversity alike."[6]

History, theology, and experience all reinforce the priority Cicero places on friendship. That is why from ancient times until the present, there always has been a future for friendship. None of us can know for certain how the drama and comedy of friendship will play out, but I'd like to suggest four cutting-edge areas in which our understanding and practice of friendship may be challenged and transformed during the twenty-first century.

Four Twenty-First-Century Friendship Projects

The Christian church has an important role to play in the twenty-first-century conversation about friendship. Here are four friendship projects I believe will impact how we practice discipleship and evangelism as this century progresses.

More Authentic and Deeper Interracial and Cross-cultural Friendships—At a recent annual session of the American Baptist Churches of New Jersey, workshop participants focused on the state of interracial friendships. Most of the European American attendees expressed pride in the progress our churches have made in fostering better relationships among the various racial, cultural, and ethnic groups found in our fellowship. However, participants from minority cultures revealed that from their perspective, only a little progress has been made and that genuine friendships across these boundaries are relatively rare.

Both groups are on to something significant. My generation (I am in my fifties) has experienced interracial and cross-cultural friendships on a much grander scale than the generation of our parents. And when I observe the friendship circle patterns of today's young adults (18–35-year-olds), I can't help but notice a greater tendency to befriend people from all sorts of different backgrounds. However, there is also much more work to be done in fostering authentic cross-cultural friendships and intentionally multicultural communities in our churches, neighborhoods, and world.

Since its inception, the church has struggled with cross-cultural relational issues (see Acts 6 and 15). In today's multicultural and post-segregated world, the church needs to foster ministries of discipleship in which friendships spanning such boundaries are modeled and encouraged. How do we encourage people to open up their close friendship circles to people of other races and cultures? How does the church create an environment where these friendships can inform our study of Scripture, our devotional and worship experiences, and our outreach?[7]

Interfaith Friendships Where Convictions and Acceptance Coexist—How should dedicated adherents of different religions relate to one another? Is friendship desirable or possible?

Speaking as a committed Christian who fervently believes in the mandate of the Great Commission, I do not accept the oft-expressed view that peaceful coexistence between people of differing religions depends upon everyone's willingness to sacrifice their convictions about exclusive truth. Instead, I believe our communities are strengthened as we learn to talk about those areas in which we disagree. For some, the prospect of having a friend from another faith is difficult to imagine. The clash of truth claims drowns out the possibility of close sharing and love. For others, the imperative to promote reconciliation and understanding trumps exclusivist doctrines. In chapter seven, I argue for a middle ground in which the two innermost circles of friendship are reserved for people who support our faith journeys, and invite people with significant religious differences only into circles three and four.

How do we practice interfaith friendships where convictions and acceptance coexist? The following principles could help create an environment where convictions can be honestly shared and friendships maintained even when differences persist:

- All people have the right to choose and practice their religion freely without governmental or cultural persecution or sanction.
- People of faith have the right to share their religious, philosophical, and political convictions through peaceful means, and to engage in serious dialogue with people from other religions as we search for truth about God and mutual understanding.
- It is never permissible, moral, or ethical to employ manipulation, violence, threats, or coercion in promoting one's religion.
- When disagreements surface, we must maintain respect toward members of other religions and beliefs.
- When common concerns are identified, people of different faiths can work together on those issues without denying their differences in other areas.

Imagine if Christians agreed to these guiding ideals in dialogue with people of other faiths and with those of no religious conviction at all! We could question those with differing worldviews, learn from one another, and together make a transformative difference in God's world.

Equality in Friendship between Women and Men—Also in chapter seven, I outlined how men and women may enter into and practice platonic friendship in a way that honors Christian standards of decorum, morality, and ethics. Michael Monsour maintains that female-male friendships serve as a "buffer against loneliness in every stage of the life span" and so "should no longer be considered relational anomalies, aberrations, or functionally identical to same-sex friendships."[8] He contends that the twenty-first century will be a period in which male-female friendships will become much more commonplace, in part because of women's expanding presence in the workplace and the increase in Internet-based social relationships.[9]

We can no longer seek to address the relational health of congregations without taking male-female friendships into account. The increasing numbers of female clergy and professional women in the workplace necessitates the rethinking of certain church practices. Gone are the days when male deacons can exercise exclusive spiritual oversight of a congregation's life, while deaconesses merely prepare communion. Shared leadership and full equality between men and women are essential for congregations that seek to attract and disciple half of the human population.

Churches may also need to reconsider the role of gender-specific small groups (such as the traditional men's and women's ministries). Single-gender groups may have made sense in an era when societal roles in general were largely gender-segregated. However, in the twenty-first century, many spouses prefer to be in small-group settings with their partners, and not apart from them. Following Jesus' example, churches should validate male-female friendships and provide sound advice for their members, so that they might manage these relationships in a thoroughly moral and ethical manner.

Friendship as a Force for Peace—Jesus declares, "Blessed are the peacemakers, for they will be called children of God" (Matthew 5:9). Paul says, "If it is possible, so far as it depends on you, live at peace with all" (Romans 12:18). Peter admonishes us to "seek peace and pursue it" (1 Peter 3:11). Friendship is the ultimate expression of peace between people. When we share the good news of Jesus Christ, we invite others into God's kingdom of peace (John 20:21). In this kingdom, even enemies become friends:

> But now in Christ Jesus you who once were far off have been brought near by the blood of Christ. For he is our peace; in his flesh he has made both groups into one and has broken down the dividing wall, that is, the hostility between us. He has abolished the law with its commandments and ordinances, that he might create in himself one new humanity in place of the two, thus making peace, and might reconcile both groups to God in one body through the cross, thus putting to death that hostility through it. So he came and proclaimed peace to you who were far off and peace to those who were near; for through him both of us have access in one Spirit to the Father. So then you are no longer strangers and aliens, but you are citizens with the saints and also members of the household of God. (Ephesians 2:13-19)

The biblical vision of peace extends from God's people into the entire world. In Isaiah's messianic prophecy, "The wolf shall live with the lamb, the leopard shall lie down with the kid, the calf and the lion and the fatling together, and a little child shall lead them" (Isaiah 11:6). Israel and its two great enemies (Egypt and Assyria) will be connected together not just by a physical road, but also by a common acknowledgment of God (Isaiah 19:19-25). Friendship with God will foster friendship among nations.

Churches, denominations, other organizations, and even nations create and maintain friendship circles in much the same way individuals do. We often hear, for example, that the United States and the United Kingdom share a special and close friendship. Other countries are isolated and have few friends in the world. In the twenty-first century, concerns about terrorism, the renewal of the nuclear arms race, and global economic inequalities are just some of the stressors that alienate nations and cultures from one another and work against peaceful coexistence.

The peacemaking ministry of the Christian church is as necessary in this century as any other. If Isaiah could catch a prophetic vision of Egypt, Assyria, and Israel living as friends, don't we have permission to dream of reconciling contemporary enemies in the name of Christ? Christians in every nation should seek to enrich the friendship circles of their countries as part of their social action witness. The *friendship circles* model, when applied to international relations, reveals the strong and weak ties between countries, and thus can guide our churches as we consider various bridge-building initiatives.

A Final Meditation: God's Love and Friendship

Jesus says, "No one has greater love than this, to lay down one's life for one's friends" (John 15:13). In sacrificing his life for humanity, Jesus models true friendship and provides the only authentic foundation for the church's evangelism and discipleship ministries.

The good news is that Jesus is our friend, and through his loving sacrifice we are offered salvation. In laying down his life, Jesus demonstrates how his followers are to live. Disciples express God's love for others by sacrificing their lives in the name of Christ: "If any want to become my followers, let them deny themselves and take up their cross daily and follow me" (Luke 9:23).

Both evangelism and discipleship are expressions of divine friendship. Evangelism offers God's friendship to a world drowning in loneliness. Discipleship is a journey into the mystery of an ever-deepening friendship with God that is made possible through Christ.

Love is the wellspring of friendship. Love inspires us to invite others into our friendship circles. Love keeps our friends in our circles. Love is the precious gift we receive from our friends who are in our circles. Love overcomes all fears (1 John 4:18) and banishes loneliness from our hearts, as we surround ourselves with faithful circles of friends.

APPENDIX

Circles of Friendship Exercises[1]

Each of the following exercises provided here may be found on www.judsonpress.com under the Free Downloads menu. The PDFs offer larger graphics for easier completion and reproduction.

1. Exercises 1 and 2 were originally published in Lee B. Spitzer, *Endless Possibilities: A Spiritual Journey Course Book* (Mercerville, NJ: Spiritual Journey Press, 2001), 92–93.

EXERCISE 1

Jesus' Friendship Circles

Jesus gathered friends and others around him with wisdom and insight. In chapter two, I shared my own snapshot depicting Jesus' Friendship Circles. I chose to picture the key relationships Jesus had at the time of his ride into Jerusalem on Palm Sunday. Now it's your turn.

Read John 15:1-17. Then fill in the Friendship Circles at right, showing how close the people listed below were to Jesus' heart as he prepared to face the cross. (Note: If you prefer, you can choose another moment in Jesus' life, and depict his friendships at that time.)

- His mother, Mary
- Peter, James, and John
- Judas
- The other 8 apostles
- Mary, her sister, Martha, and their brother, Lazarus
- The Jerusalem crowds
- Those unnamed disciples who later joined the apostles in the upper room
- Nicodemus
- The Pharisees and Sadducees
- John the Baptist
- Jesus' father, Joseph, and siblings

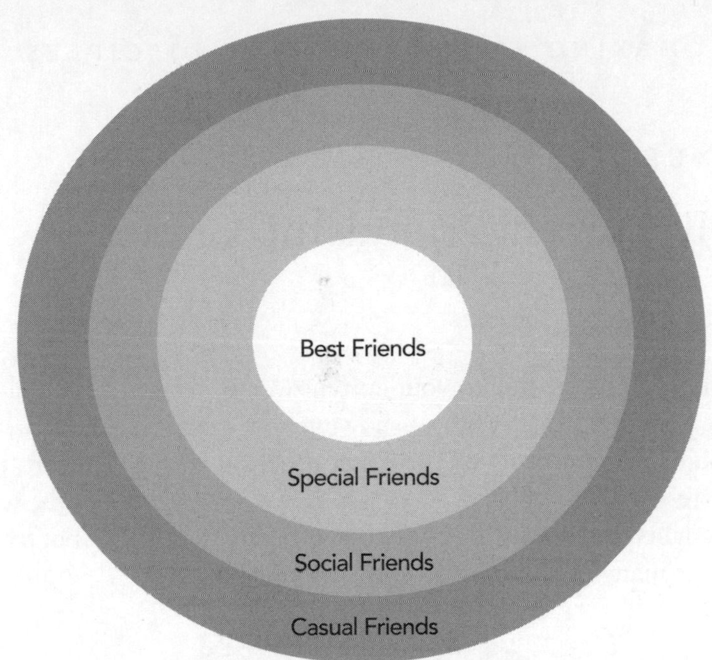

Key to Placing People in the Friendship Circles

1. Best Friends (center circle or bull's-eye): the 2 or 3 dearest loved ones.

2. Special Friends: the 3–5 closest friends outside the center circle.

3. Social Friends: the 7–12 people one spends a great deal of time with.

4. Casual Friends: the 50–200 people one knows by name and might socialize or work with (acquaintances).

Outside the Circles: Non-friends and enemies.

Jesus' Circle of Friends on ______________________________

EXERCISE 2

My Current Friendship Circles

Where do others fit into your current web of relationships? Fill in the Friendship Circles below, showing how close individuals are to you at the present time. The closer a person is to your heart, the more potential influence he or she has over your emotions, will, thoughts, and actions. In circle four, groups can be listed, but try to list as many significant individuals as possible.

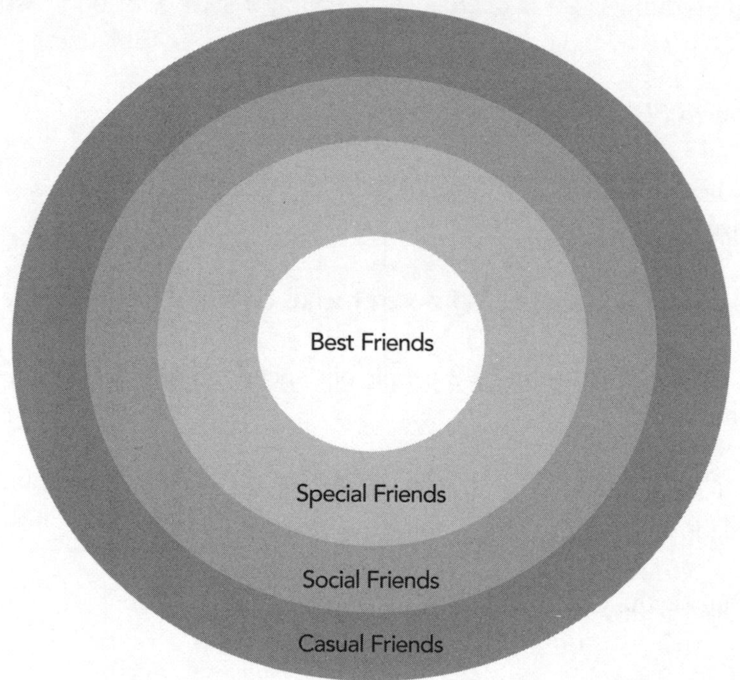

My Circle of Friends as of ____________________ (today's date)

EXERCISE 3

My Current Friendship Circles—By Groupings

Individuals in our web of relationships share connections with others. Review your answers to exercise 2 and fill in the Friendship Circles below, keeping individuals in the appropriate circles but also placing them in the "slices" that best describe their relationships with you—family friends, church friends, work friends, neighbors, non-local friends, and others (you also can create custom categories).

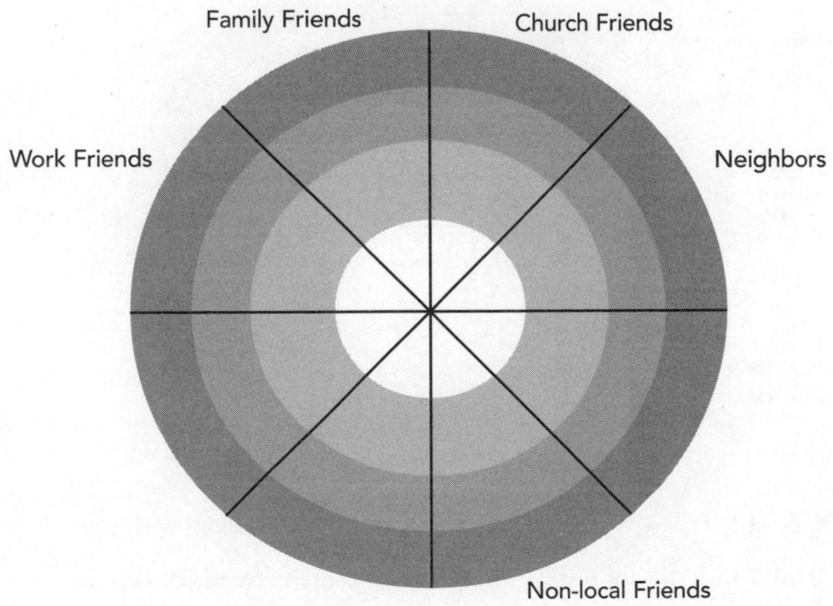

My Circle of Friends as of ____________________ (today's date)

EXERCISE 4

My Current Friendship Circles and Social Networking Sites

Social networking sites are dramatically expanding the number of people with whom we keep in touch. Review your answers to exercise 2 and fill in the Friendship Circles below. If a friend is networked to you (through Facebook or other sites) place them in the top half of the circle; if not, place them in the bottom half. What do you see?

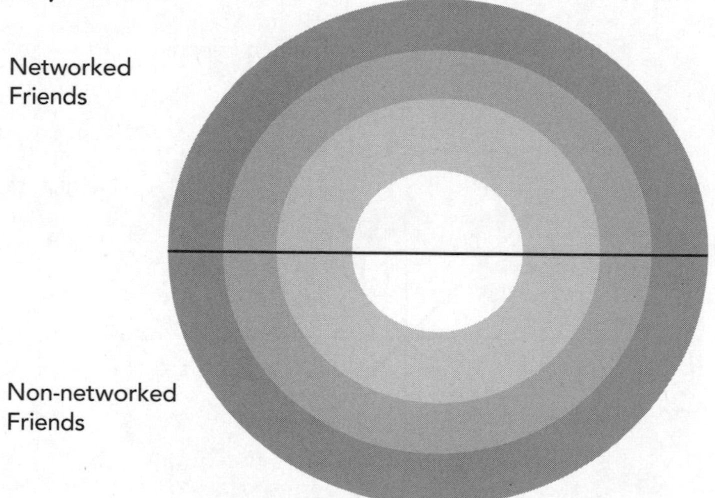

CIRCLE 1: ___ of my ___ *Best Friends* are networked with me.

CIRCLE 2: ___ of my ___ *Special Friends* are networked with me.

CIRCLE 3: ___ of my ___ *Social Friends* are networked with me.

CIRCLE 4: ___ of my ___ *Casual Friends* are networked with me.

EXERCISE 5

Social Networking Sites and My Online Web of Relationships

Building on the results from exercise 4, this exercise focuses on grouping the people with whom you are networked through various social networking websites. We'll assume you are analyzing your Facebook "Friends," but you can adapt this exercise to other sites you use.

STEP 1: On Facebook, go to your Wall and look for the Friends Box on the left panel. How many total Facebook Friends do you have? ________ people

STEP 2: Click the "Friends" link at the top of your Wall. You will see 50 friends on each web page.

STEP 3: Go through the list of all of your "Friends." (You might want to print out the list so that you can complete this step in writing.) Consider your relationship with each person in your list. Next to each name, assign one of the codes from the table on the following page to indicate if the person is in one of your friendship circles, or related to you in another way or for another reason.

STEP 4: Count how many people are in each category. (A simple spreadsheet can automate this process for you.) Then write the totals and calculate percentages using the table on page 152.

STEP 5: What does the table reveal about your Facebook "Friends" and your friendship circles? Some reflection questions you might wish to answer are:

1. How many of your Facebook "Friends" are truly friends (these people are in one of your four friendship circles)?

2. How do you use Facebook to maintain and enhance your relationship with your close friends (those in the three inner circles)?

3. Do you feel that Facebook has enabled you to sustain and deepen your close friendships? Why or why not?

Code	Category	Number	Percent
(1)	Circle 1 Friends (Best Friends)		
(2)	Circle 2 Friends (Special Friends)		
(3)	Circle 3 Friends (Social Friends)		
(4)	Circle 4 Friends (Casual Friends)		
C	Church people who are not in the 4 circles		
F	Family members who are not in the 4 circles		
J	Job related people who are not in the 4 circles		
N	Neighbors/locals who are not in the 4 circles		
P	People from your past who are not in the 4 circles		
X	Ex-friends whom you prefer not to deal with		
?	People you do not know at all (this happens!)		
Totals	**Total Number of Facebook "Friends"**		**100%**

EXERCISE 6

My Current Friends and Discipleship Possibilities

Appropriate discipleship relationships depend upon discerning the spiritual maturity of others. How many of your current friends have the spiritual maturity to disciple you effectively? How many would best be described as your peers in the faith? How many could you disciple? Review your answers to exercise 2 and fill in the Friendship Circles below. What do you see?

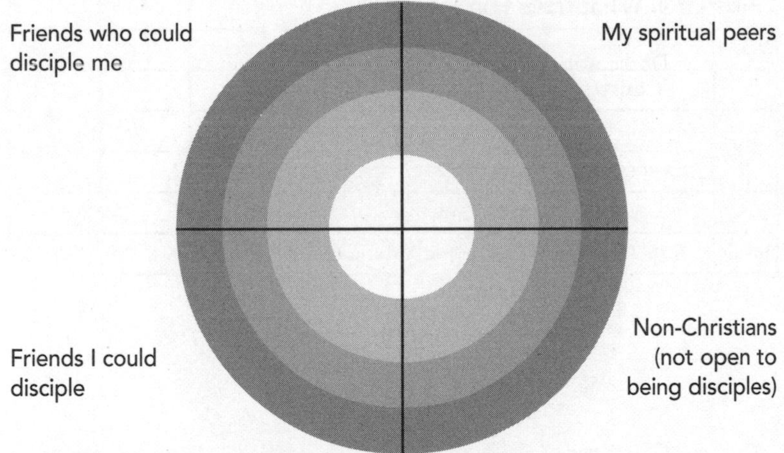

Where do the majority of your friends fall?

____

What group has the most people in your three inner circles?

____

EXERCISE 7

My Current Friends and Their Faith

Friendship evangelism depends upon faith diversity in your web of relationships. How many of your current friends are Christians? Review your answers to exercise 2 and fill in the friendship circles below. Distinguish between friends who are dedicated Christians (a personal relationship with Christ), cultural Christians (occasionally go to church but faith isn't a central to their lives), and non-Christians. What have you learned?

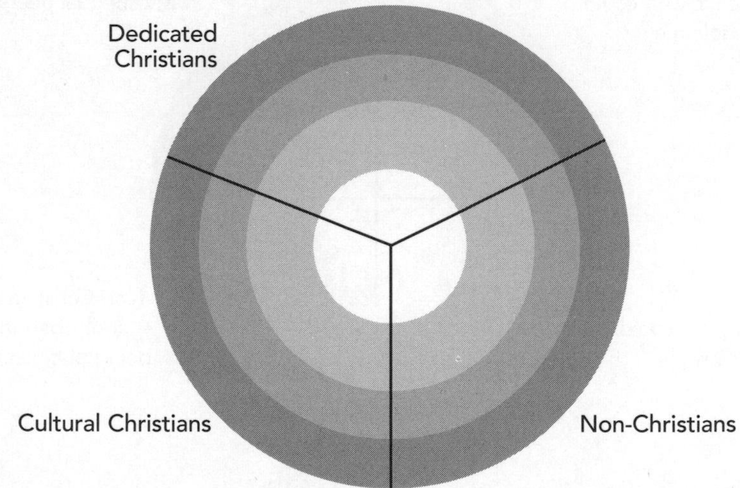

Where do most of your friends fall?

____

What group has the most people in your three inner circles?

____

EXERCISE 8

My Friendship Circles before My Last Major Life Change

Think back to a time right before your last major life change (moving, starting of a new job, getting married or divorced). Who were the individuals in your web of relationships? Fill in the friendship circles below, showing how close individuals were to you at that time. The closer a person is to your heart, the more potential influence over you. In Circle 4, groups can be listed, but list as many significant individuals as possible.

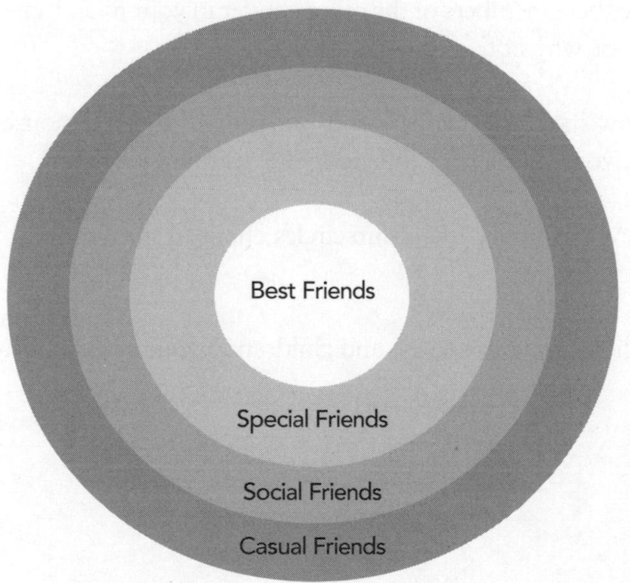

My Circle of Friends as of ______________________________

EXERCISE 9

Friendship Circles Exercise Reflection

Having completed the friendship circles exercised, take some time to reflect on any insights you may have gained from the experience by considering the following questions:

- What qualities of character and personality are found among your close friends?

- Are there members of the other gender in your inner three circles? Why or why not?

- How have your close friends influenced your relationship with God, your ministry or job, and your spiritual journeys?

- How have your friendship circles changed since moving to your current locale?

- Where are your spouse and children in your circles? Why?

Notes

Introduction

1. Albert-László Barabási, *Linked: How Everything Is Connected to Everything Else and What It Means for Business, Science, and Everyday Life* (New York: A Plume Book, Penguin Group, 2003), 39.

2. Jessica E. Vascellaro, "Facebook Cites Rapid Growth in Users, Cash Flow," *The Wall Street Journal*, September 16, 2009, B4.

3. Adin Steinsaltz, *Simple Words: Thinking About What Really Matters in Life* (New York: Simon and Shuster, Inc., 1999), 159.

4. Henry David Thoreau, *Friendship* (Elibron Classics Replica Edition © 2005. New York: Thomas Y. Crowell and Company, 1906), 13–14.

5. Steinsaltz, 161.

6. Ibid., 165.

7. Thoreau, 15.

8. Ibid.

9. Steinsaltz, 170.

Chapter 1

1. Allan Bloom, *Love and Friendship* (New York: Simon and Schuster, 1993), 14.

2. Ibid.

3. John T. Cacioppo and William Patrick, *Loneliness: Human Nature and the Need for Social Connection* (New York: W.W. Norton, 2008), 4–5.

4. Sara Vogan, *Loss of Flight* (New York: Bantam Books, 1989), 6.

5. Cacioppo and Patrick. 228.

6. C.S. Lewis, *The Four Loves* (San Diego: Harcourt Brace Jovanovich, Publishers, 1960), 12.

7. Letty Cottin Pogrebin, *Among Friends: Who We Like, Why We Like Them, and What We Do with Them* (New York: McGraw-Hill Book Company, 1987), 3.

8. Ibid., 6.

9. Cacioppo and Patrick, 80.

10. See Lee B. Spitzer, *Endless Possibilities: Exploring the Jour-neys of Your Life* (Mercerville, NJ: Spiritual Journey Press, 1997).

11. Shusaku Endo, *A Life of Jesus*, trans. Richard A. Schuchert (Tokyo: Charles E. Tuttle Company, 1973, 1978), 119 (emphasis mine).

Chapter 2

1. Elie Wiesel, *The Time of the Uprooted,* trans. David Hapgood (New York: Alfred A. Knopf, 2005), 134.
2. Endo, 54.
3. Ibid., 80.
4. Ibid.
5. Ibid., 174.
6. See John Burns, *Modeling Mary in Christian Discipleship* (Valley Forge, PA: Judson Press, 2007).

Chapter 3

1. Cynthia Ozick, *Metaphor and Memory* (New York: Vintage International, Random House, 1991), 253.
2. Ibid., 263–64.
3. C. G. Jung, *Answer to Job,* trans. R.F.C. Hull (Princeton, NJ: Princeton University Press, 1973), 14.
4. See Lee B. Spitzer, *Jesus Christ from Cover to Cover: Tracing the Messianic Journey from Genesis to Revelation* (Mercerville, NJ: Spiritual Journey Press, 2006), 182–87, for a more extended treatment of this theme.

Chapter 4

1. Alan Loy McGinnis, *The Friendship Factor: How to Get Closer to the People You Care For* (Minneapolis: Augsburg Fortress Publishers, 2004), 2.
2. Rosemary Blieszner and Rebecca G. Adams, *Adult Friendship* (Newbury Park, CA: Sage Publications, Inc., 1992), 62.
3. Oscar Niemeyer, *The Curves of Time: The Memoirs of Oscar Niemeyer,* trans. Izabel Murat Burbridge (London: Phaidon Press Limited, 2000), 176.
4. Aristotle, *The Nichomachean Ethics,* revised edition, trans. J.A.K. Thompson (London: Penguin Books Ltd., 2006), 203.
5. Ibid., 204.
6. Ibid., 205.
7. Ibid.
8. Elizabeth O'Connor, *Call to Commitment: The Story of the Church of the Savior, Washington, D.C.* (New York: Harper and Row, Publishers, 1963), 93–94.
9. Quoted in Elizabeth O'Connor, *Servant Leaders, Servant Structures* (Washington, DC: The Servant Leadership School, 1991), 7.

Chapter 5

1. Ray Pahl, *On Friendship* (Cambridge: Polity Press, 2000), 2.
2. Ibid., 3.
3. Ibid., 12.
4. Ibid., 61.

5. William K. Rawlins, *The Compass of Friendship: Narratives, Identities and Dialogues* (Los Angeles: Sage Publications, Inc., 2009), 1.

6. Robin Dunbar, *Grooming, Gossip, and the Evolution of Language* (Cambridge, MA: Harvard University Press, 1998), 69–77.

7. Ibid., 76–77.

8. Pahl, 9.

9. Blieszner and Adams, 46–47.

10. Ibid.

11. Ibid., 48.

12. Dunbar, 76.

13. See Lee B. Spitzer, *Love, Friendship and Mission: Missionary Friendship Circles Report* (Mercerville, NJ: Spiritual Journey Press, 2009), 50–52.

Chapter 6

1. Rebecca G. Adams and Graham Allan, eds., *Placing Friendship in Context* (Cambridge: Cambridge University Press, 1998), 3–4 (original emphasis).

2. Ibid., 7–9.

3. Blieszner and Adams, 115.

4. Ibid., 115–16.

5. Rawlins, 7–10.

6. The *Endless Possibilities Health and Faithfulness Survey* materials may be accessed on the ABCNJ regional website at www.abcnj.net/ministries/health-and-faithfulness.

Chapter 7

1. This section's discussion is based on two key articles by Mark S. Granovetter: "The Strength of Weak Ties," *The American Journal of Sociology*, Vol. 78, No. 6 (May 1973): 1360–80, and "The Strength of Weak Ties: A Network Theory Revisited," *Sociological Theory*, Volume 1 (1983): 201–33. For a more general discussion of the issue of ties between people, which is often referred to as the small world problem, see: Jeffrey Travers and Stanley Milgram, "An Experimental Study of the Small World Problem," *Sociometry* 32, no. 4 (Dec. 1969): 425–43, and Duncan J. Watts, *Six Degrees: The Science of a Conected Age* (New York: W.W. Norton and Company, Inc., 2003).

2. Blieszner and Adams, 9–12.

3. See note 1 above.

4. J.R.R. Tolkien, *The Letters of J.R.R. Tolkien*, ed. Humphrey Carpenter with the assistance of Christopher Tolkien (New York: Houghton Mifflin Company, 2000), 48.

5. Kathy Werking, *We're Just Good Friends: Women and Men in Nonromantic Relationships* (New York: The Guilford Press, 1997), 30–31.

6. Ibid., 135–40.

7. Ibid., 140.

8. Ibid., 68.

Chapter 8

1. Aelred of Rievaulx, *Spiritual Friendship,* trans. Mary Eugenia Laker (Kalamazoo, MI: Cistercian Publications, 1977), 53.

2. For a brief description of the classical spiritual journey paradigm, see Lee B. Spitzer, *Endless Possibilities: Exploring the Journeys of Your Life*, 115–17.

3. Aelred, 74–75.

4. Ibid., 105.

5. This section is based on Lee B. Spitzer, *Endless Possibilities: Exploring the Journeys of Your Life*, 3–25.

6. Rawlins, 47.

7. Ibid.

8. Elizabeth O'Connor, *Servant Leaders, Servant Structures*, 90.

9. L. Gregory Jones and Kevin R. Armstrong, *Resurrecting Excellence: Shaping Faithful Christian Ministry* (Grand Rapids: William B. Eerdmans Publishing Company, 2006), 8.

10. Ibid., 59.

11. Ibid., 65.

12. Ibid., 74.

Chapter 9

1. Henri J.M. Nouwen, *The Genesee Diary: Report from a Trappist Monastery* (Garden City, NY: Image Books, 1981), 177.

2. Dorothy Day, *The Long Loneliness* (Garden City, NY: Image Books, 1959), 45.

3. Ibid., 49.

4. Ibid., 276–77.

5. Thomas Merton, *Contemplation in a World of Action* (Garden City, NY: Image Books, 1971), 178–79.

6. Thomas Merton, *Life and Holiness* (Garden City, NY: Image Books, A Division of Doubleday and Company, Inc., 1963), 9.

7. Henri Nouwen, *The Way of the Heart: Desert Spirituality and Contemporary Ministry* (New York: The Seabury Press, 1981), 69.

8. Ibid., 39.

9. Bliesner and Adams, 12–13.

10. Robert D. Putnam, *Bowling Alone: The Collapse and Revival of American Community* (New York: Simon and Schuster Paperbacks, 2000), 27. See also Miller McPherson, Lynn Smith-Lovin, and Matthew E. Brashears, "Social Isolation in America: Changes in Core Discussion Networks Over Two Decades." *American Sociological Review* 71 (June 2006): 353–75.

11. Putnam, *Bowling Alone*, 71–72.

Chapter 10

1. Edward Young, *The Poetical Works of Edward Young*, vol. II (London: William Pickering, 1844), 76.

2. Edmond Rostand, *Cyrano de Bergerac*, trans. Carol Clark (London: Penguin Books, 2005), 184.

3. Beverley Fehr, *Friendship Processes* (Thousand Oaks, CA: Sage Publications, 1996), 187–97.

4. Pogrebin, 103–04.

5. Ibid., 104.

Conclusion

1. Daniel Schwartz, *Aquinas on Friendship* (Oxford: Oxford University Press, 2007), 14.

2. Ibid.

3. Ibid., 107.

4. Ibid.

5. Michael Ford, *Wounded Prophet: A Portrait of Henri J. M. Nouwen* (New York: Image Books, 2002), 106.

6. Cicero, *On the Good Life*, trans. Michael Grant (London: Penguin Books, 1971), 185.

7. See Curtiss Paul DeYoung, *Coming Together in the 21st Century: The Bible's Message in an Age of Diversity* (Judson Press, 2009) for more scholarship, scriptural insight, and practical strategies for making this happen.

8. Michael Monsour, *Women and Men as Friends: Relationships Across the Life Span in the 21st Century* (Mahwah, NJ: Lawrence Earlbaum Associates, 2002), xiv.

9. Ibid., 1.

Lisa Marie Rice

Woman on the Run

Ellora's Cave
Romantica Publishing

An Ellora's Cave Romantica Publication

www.ellorascave.com

Woman on the Run

ISBN #1419952056

Edited by: Marty Klopfenstein
Cover art by: Syneca

Electronic book Publication: September, 2004
Trade paperback Publication: October, 2005

Warning:

The following material contains graphic sexual content meant for mature readers. *Woman on the Run* has been rated *S-ensuous* by a minimum of three independent reviewers.

Ellora's Cave Publishing offers three levels of Romantica™ reading entertainment: S (S-ensuous), E (E-rotic), and X (X-treme).

S-*ensuous* love scenes are explicit and leave nothing to the imagination.

E-*rotic* love scenes are explicit, leave nothing to the imagination, and are high in volume per the overall word count. In addition, some E-rated titles might contain fantasy material that some readers find objectionable, such as bondage, submission, same sex encounters, forced seductions, etc. E-rated titles are the most graphic titles we carry; it is common, for instance, for an author to use words such as "fucking", "cock", "pussy", etc., within their work of literature.

X-*treme* titles differ from E-rated titles only in plot premise and storyline execution. Unlike E-rated titles, stories designated with the letter X tend to contain controversial subject matter not for the faint of heart.

Also by Lisa Marie Rice:

Christmas Angel
Midnight Man
Midnight Run
Port Of Paradise